LETTERHEAD & LOGO DESIGN [9]

ROCKPORT

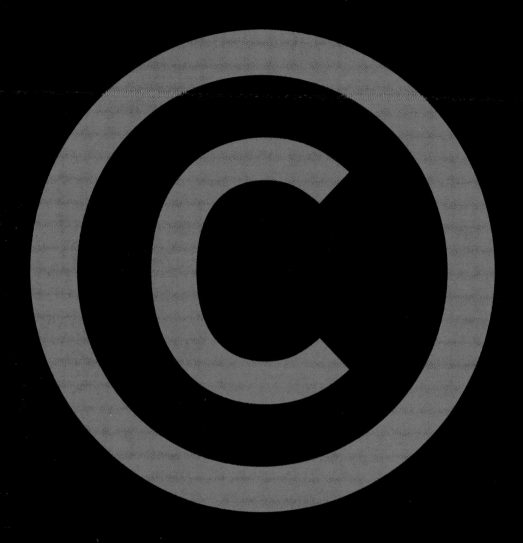

First published in the
United States of America by
Rockport Publishers, a member
of Quayside Publishing Group
100 Cummings Center
Suite 406-L
Beverly, Massachusetts
01915-6101
Telephone: (978) 282-9590
Fax: (978) 283-2742
www.rockpub.com

Printed in China

ISBN-13: 978-1-59253-389-3
ISBN-10: 1-59253-389-2

10 9 8 7 6 5 4

Design: MINE™
www.minesf.com

Opposite: "9 Lives" logo
Firm: Blackdog
Designer/Illustrator: Mark Fox
Art Director: Jeff Carino
Client: Eveready Battery Co.
Agency: Landor

LETTERHEAD & LOGO DESIGN⁹

LETTERHEAD & LOGO DESIGN⁹

BEVERLY MASSACHUSETTS

ROCKPORT PUBLISHERS

TOC

ALABAMA
ALASKA
CALIFORNIA
COLORADO
CONNECTICUT
FLORIDA
GEORGIA
HAWAII
ILLINOIS
INDIANA
IOWA
KANSAS
KENTUCKY
LOUISIANA
MARYLAND
MASSACHUSETTS
MICHIGAN
MINNESOTA
MONTANA
MISSOURI
NEBRASKA
NEVADA
NEW JERSEY
NEW MEXICO
NEW YORK
NORTH CAROLINA
OHIO
OREGON
PENNSYLVANIA
RHODE ISLAND
SOUTH CAROLINA
TENNESSEE
TEXAS
UTAH
VERMONT
VIRGINIA
WASHINGTON
WISCONSIN

0   100   200   300   400   500   600

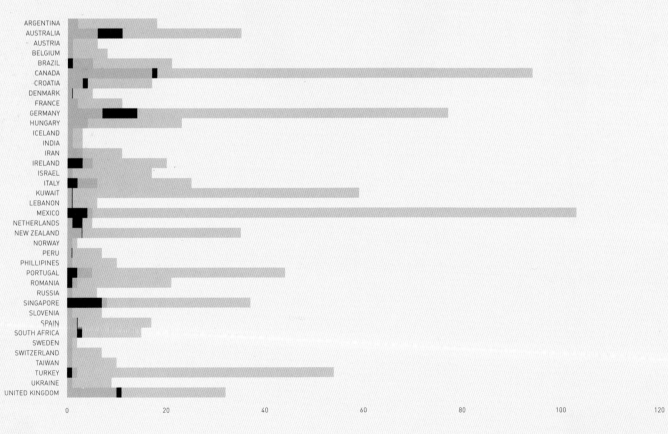

ARGENTINA
AUSTRALIA
AUSTRIA
BELGIUM
BRAZIL
CANADA
CROATIA
DENMARK
FRANCE
GERMANY
HUNGARY
ICELAND
INDIA
IRAN
IRELAND
ISRAEL
ITALY
KUWAIT
LEBANON
MEXICO
NETHERLANDS
NEW ZEALAND
NORWAY
PERU
PHILLIPINES
PORTUGAL
ROMANIA
RUSSIA
SINGAPORE
SLOVENIA
SPAIN
SOUTH AFRICA
SWEDEN
SWITZERLAND
TAIWAN
TURKEY
UKRAINE
UNITED KINGDOM

0   20   40   60   80   100   120

BY THE NUMBERS: SUBMITTING FIRMS   SUBMITTED ENTRIES   SELECTED ENTRIES

The wonderful thing about design

The wonderful thing about design is its diversity, its individuality. For every problem there are an infinite number of solutions. In the face of such inestimable quantity, however, successful design is nonetheless a qualitative experience—one in which context is as important as content, and for which concept trumps all. How then, does one go about assembling a collection of design work, and presenting it in a way that is both meaningful and informative?

In compiling this book, we considered origin, intent, and authenticity as qualifying factors (in addition, of course, to an underlying commitment to graphic excellence). We received more than 3,000 submissions, contributed from 38 U.S. states and 40 countries. Of these, some 300 are presented here as representative of the best work being done in their respective localities. To better present the solutions, they are collated based on their qualitative attributes, rather than being organized simply by client type or industry. As you review this book, consider the work both individually and collectively. Each entry is included for its own merit, but each spread and each section also contains its own, secondary, narrative. We hope that it will inform, entertain, inspire, and enlighten.

Enjoy.

The Author

Christopher Simmons is a designer, writer, and educator. His passion and interest in exploring the increasingly complex notion of identity has lead him to develop and teach courses on the subject at the California College of the Arts and San Francisco's Academy of Art University. An advocate for the power of design, he also lectures at colleges, universities, and professional associations on topics ranging from collaborative work models and the role of language in graphic design to issues of professional, ethical, and sustainable practice. His first book, *Logo Lab*, was released in June 2005. Christopher is the president of the San Francisco chapter of the American Institute of Graphic Arts (AIGA).

In 2004, Christopher launched his own independent design office, affectionately named MINE™.

MINE was founded with the philosophy that good design is good business, and that working smart beats working big. A multidisciplinary studio, MINE offers innovative and informed solutions as tools to support corporate, enterprise, and nonprofit organizations. Emphasizing intelligence-based design and sound strategic thinking, MINE seeks to create definitive, stand-out work that projects a unique position of leadership and promotes the highest standards of excellence.

1

2

3

PREVIOUS PAGE | **MINE™** | DESIGNER/ART DIRECTOR **CHRISTOPHER SIMMONS** | ILLUSTRATOR **NATHAN WILSON**
1   **FREE SPEECH** | DESIGNER **CHRISTOPHER SIMMONS** | PROMOTIONAL T-SHIRT GRAPHIC
2   **CERTIFIED VEGAN** | DESIGNER **CHRISTOPHER SIMMONS** | LOGO TO IDENTIFY CERTIFIED VEGAN FOODS
3   **RED DEVILS** | DESIGNER **CHRISTOPHER SIMMONS** | INDEPENDENT SOCCER TEAM LOGO

$$\left(L + M \right)^{P}$$

The Power of Partnership

ACADEMY FRESNO

1   LABOR MANAGEMENT PARTNERSHIP* | DESIGNER **CHRISTOPHER SIMMONS** | INITIATIVE TO UNIFY THE MANAGEMENT AND UNIONS OF KAISER PERMANENTE
2   VISUAL QUICKPROJECT | DESIGNER **CHRISTOPHER SIMMONS** | INSTRUCTIONAL BOOK SERIES, PEACHPIT PRESS
3   HARTMAN GRIFFIN ASSOCIATES* | DESIGNERS **CHRISTOPHER SIMMONS, AMBER REED** | MONOGRAM FOR AN INDEPENDENT DEVELOPMENT CONSULTANT
4   ACADEMY FRESNO* | DESIGNER **CHRISTOPHER SIMMONS** | CREST FOR A PUBLIC COLLEGE PREPARATORY SCHOOL
    * PROJECT DESIGNED WHILE A PRINCIPAL AT ALTERPOP, PRIOR TO FOUNDING MINE™

1

2

3

NUEVA WAVE

1   **COMIRA** | DESIGNER **CHRISTOPHER SIMMONS** | COMPUTER-BASED TESTING PROVIDER
2   **RICH STEEL** | DESIGNER **CHRISTOPHER SIMMONS** | TRAVEL WRITER
3   **NEUVA WAVE** | DESIGNER **CHRISTOPHER SIMMONS** | SPORTS TEAM LOGO FOR A PRIVATE SCHOOL
     FACING PAGE | **PARADOX MEDIA** | DESIGNER. **CHRISTOPHER SIMMONS** | LOGO AND STATIONERY FOR AN EVENT PRODUCTION COMPANY

PARADOX
PRODUCTION PROMOTION DESIGN

JUSTIN KATZ
JUSTIN@PARADOXMEDIA.BIZ
510.506.2210

PARADOX MEDIA
PO BOX 3974
BERKELEY CA 94703

PARADOX
PRODUCTION PROMOTION DESIGN

Beauty: The grace of nature, the elegance of a curve, the harmony or tension realized through an inspired sense of proportion or scale. From the nostalgic vernacular of a Havana street scene to the sleek functionality of a contemporary transmittal, we found beauty here in a pleasing variety of its infinite forms.

1

bar

2

3

1   FIREFLY STUDIO PTE LTD | ART DIRECTORS JAE SOH, NORMAN LAI | DESIGNERS JAE SOH, JAS SOH | CLIENT O BAR
2   PARAGON MARKETING COMMUNICATIONS | ART DIRECTOR LOUAI ALASFAHANI | DESIGNER KHALID AL RIFAE | CLIENT DEVELOPMENT ENTERPRISES
3   NOON | ART DIRECTOR CINTHIA WEN | DESIGNER ELLEN MALINOWSKI | CLIENT ICG

1

coupling

2

HEALTH
FIRST™

3

nine (GALLERY)

1   COLOUR MOVIE | ART DIRECTORS MICHELLE HAMMOND, BRANDON MARTINEZ | DESIGNER FIEL VALDEZ | CLIENT NBC
2   WOW! BRANDING | ART DIRECTOR PERRY CHUA | DESIGNER WILL JOHNSON | CLIENT HEALTH FIRST NETWORK
3   EMPIRE DESIGN STUDIO | ART DIRECTOR GARY TOOTH | DESIGNER CARRIE HAMILTON | CLIENT RALPH PUCCI
     FACING PAGE | OCTAVO DESIGN | ART DIRECTOR GARY DOMONEY | CLIENT KEY FINANCIAL GROUP

key financial group pty ltd abn 45 725 818 185
187 ferrars st southbank victoria 3205 australia
telephone 03 9696 4411 info@keyfinancial.com.au
facsimile 03 9696 4611 www.keyfinancial.com.au

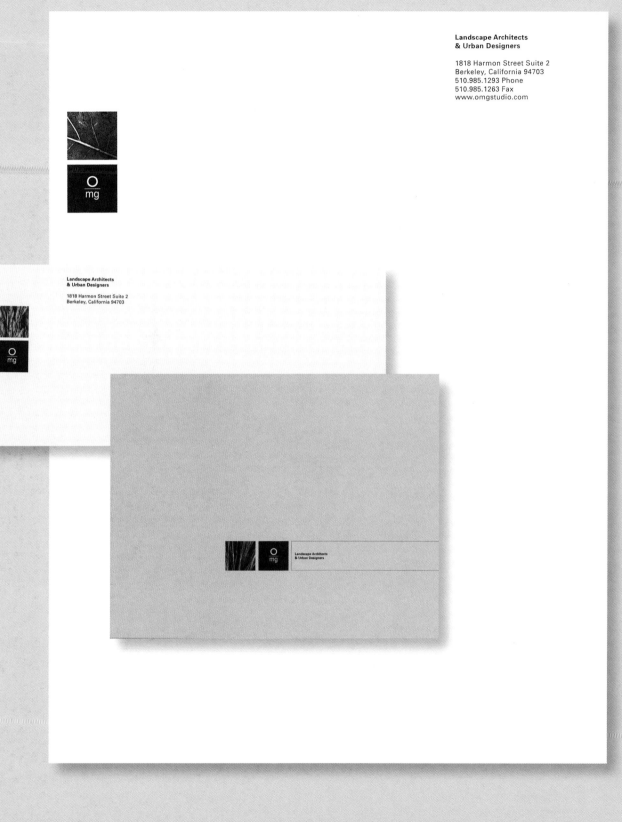

Landscape Architects
& Urban Designers

1818 Harmon Street Suite 2
Berkeley, California 94703
510.985.1293 Phone
510.985.1263 Fax
www.omgstudio.com

Landscape Architects
& Urban Designers

1818 Harmon Street Suite 2
Berkeley, California 94703

Landscape Architects
& Urban Designers

Aaron Siskind
F O U N D A T I O N

Board of Directors
Judith Jacobs
Ira Lowe
Victor Schrager
Charles Traub

Executive Director
Anne Coleman Torrey

c/o School of Visual Arts
MFA Photography
209 East 23rd Street
New York, NY 10010

www.aaronsiskind.org
info@aaronsiskind.org

Aaron Siskind
F O U N D A T I O N

c/o School of Visual Arts
MFA Photography
209 East 23rd Street
New York, NY 10010

www.aaronsiskind.org

Aaron Siskind
F O U N D A T I O N

Charles Traub
President, Board of Directors

c/o School of Visual Arts
MFA Photography
209 East 23rd Street
New York, NY 10010

212.677.8310

www.aaronsiskind.org
info@aaronsiskind.org

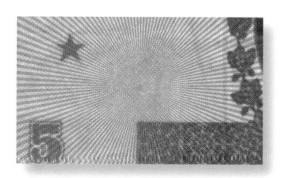

PUBLIC | ART DIRECTOR **TODD FOREMAN** | DESIGNERS **TESSA LEE, NANCY THOMAS, LINDSAY WHEELE** **HUCK'S COFFEE COMPANY**

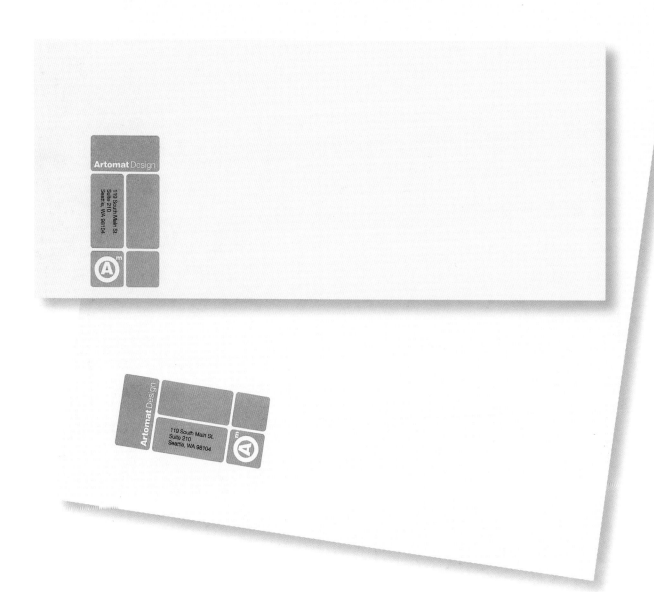

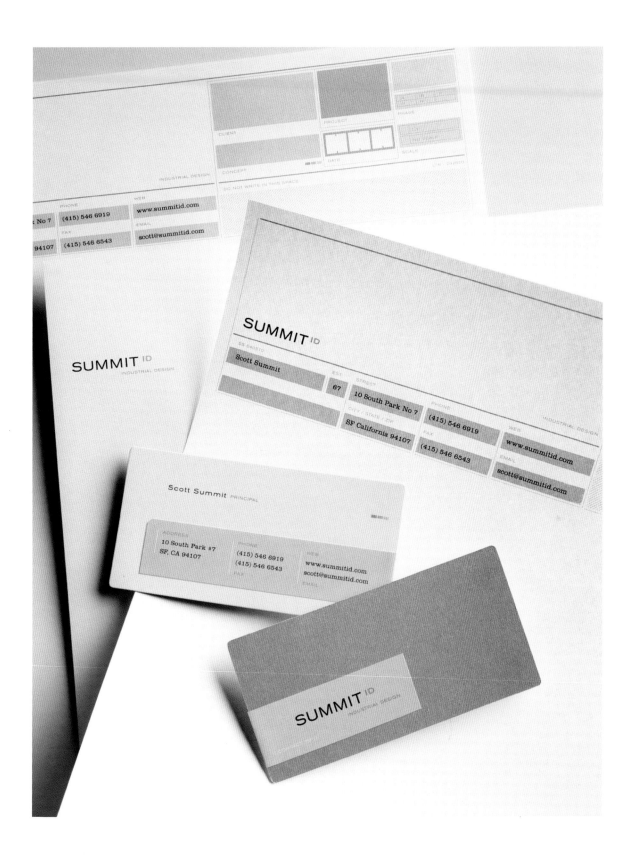

TEMPLIN BRINK DESIGN | ART DIRECTORS JOEL TEMPLIN, GABY BRINK | DESIGNER BRIAN GUNDERSON | CLIENT SUMMIT ID

NED JALBERT

AMERICAN INDIAN MASTERWORKS
57 East Main Street, Westboro, MA 01581
(508) 836-9999 voice

FACING PAGE | **MDG** | ART DIRECTOR **TIM MERRY** | DESIGNER **MIKE EATON** | CLIENT **NED JALBERT**

JOSHUA MCDONNELL | DESIGNER **JOSHUA MCDONNELL** | CLIENT **PARADISE**

Axcelerator Home Loans
We put you in control
Level 1, 150 Albert Street
South Melbourne
Victoria 3205 Australia
Telephone 03 9686 3322
Facsimile 03 9686 3518
www.axcelerator.com.au

Axcelerator Home Loans Pty Ltd
ABN 85 103 853 023. Member MIAA

OCTAVO DESIGN | ART DIRECTORS **GARY DOMONEY** | CLIENT **AXCELERATOR HOME LOANS**

The Abernathy Group

5585 Silverado Trail
Napa, CA 94558
tele: 707.738.1116
fax: 707.265.5415
lydia.mondavi@robertmondavi.com

Lydia Abernathy Mondavi
PRINCIPAL

The Abernathy Group   5585 Silverado Trail   Napa, CA 94558   tele: 707.738.1116   fax: 707.265.5415   lydia.mondavi@robertmondavi.com

THE JONES GROUP | ART DIRECTOR VICKY JONES | DESIGNER CHRIS MILLER | CLIENT THE ABERNATHY GROUP
FACING PAGE | WOW! BRANDING | ART DIRECTOR PERRY CHUA | DESIGNERS WILL JOHNSON, JEFF SCHRAMM | CLIENT PACIFIC IMPLANT INSTITUTE

PACIFIC IMPLANT *Institute*

MASTER *the Art and Science of*
IMPLANT DENTISTRY

MASTER *the Art and Science of*
IMPLANT DENTISTRY

Dr. Ron Zokol, DIRECTOR

Pacific Implant Institute
470 West Tower, City Square
555 West 12th Avenue
Vancouver, BC Canada V5Z 3X7
Phone 604.322.3209 *International* (800) 668.2280
Fax 604.322.3045 *email* ron@piidentistry.com

470 West Tower, City Square, 555 West 12th Avenue, Vancouver, BC Canada V5Z 3X7
Phone 604.322.3209 *International* (800) 668.2280 *Fax* 604.322.3045 www.piidentistry.com

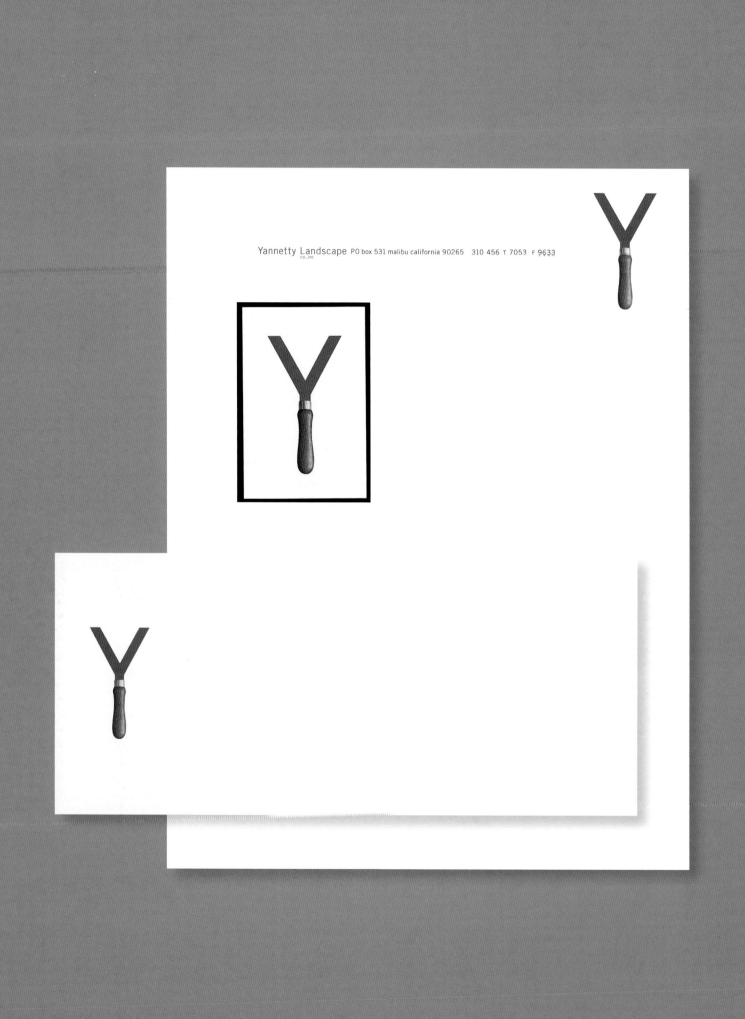

Yannetty Landscape PO box 531 malibu california 90265   310 456 T 7053 F 9633
co.,inc

**BÜ
SCHER**

**WER
NER**

**AR
CHITEK
TEN**

Büscher Werner
Architekten

BÜ
SCHER

WER
NER

AR
CHITEK
TEN

Büscher Werner
Architekten

Adelheidstraße 7
80798 München

Telefon
089 27 38 96 75
Fax
089 27 38 96 78

kontakt@
buescher-werner-
architekten.de
www.
buescher-werner-
architekten.de

Adelheidstraße 7
80798 München

Telefon
089 27 38 96 75
Fax
089 27 38 96 78

kontakt@
buescher-werner-
architekten.de
www.
buescher-werner-
architekten.de

BÜ
SCHER

WER
NER

AR
CHITEK
TEN

Büscher Werner
Architekten

FACING PAGE | **MERYL POLLEN DESIGN** | DESIGNER **MERYL POLLEN** | CLIENT **YANNETTY LANDSCAPE**
INPRAXIS, KONZEPT + GESTALTUNG | ART DIRECTORS **ANDREAS KRANZ, CHRISTIANE SCHÄFFNER** | DESIGNER **EVA MAYER**
CLIENT **WERNER BÜSCHER ARCHITECTS**

1

FONTEGRAFICA

2

1   CACAO DESIGN | ART DIRECTOR **CREATIVE TEAM** | CLIENT **FONTEGRAFICA**
2   **SIMON & GOETZ** | DESIGNER **RÜDIGER GOETZ** | CLIENT **FRANK KUHLMANN**

DAITAN

R. Maria Monteiro, 321
CEP 13025-150
Cambui Campinas SP
pabx.fax 19. 3251.3600

daitanrestaurante@terra.com.br

DAITAN

A10 DESIGN | ART DIRECTOR MARGOT TAKEDA | DESIGNER MARCELO RAMOS | CLIENT DAITAN

1

2

3

4

1 EVENSON DESIGN GROUP | ART DIRECTOR **STAN EVENSON** | DESIGNER **MARK SOJKA** | CLIENT **THE GIVING TREE**
2 GARDNER DESIGN | DESIGNER **BRIAN MILLER** | CLIENT **AIGA/LOGOLOUNGE**
3 PING-PONG DESIGN | CLIENT **MEDELLÍN SECRET**
4 MEATON DOT NET | DESIGNER **MIKE EATON** | CLIENT **BOSTON FISHSTIX**

a childrens boutique

aja&alex

Desireè Smith *Proprietor*

437 York Road • Jenkintown, Pennsylvania 19046
tel. 215.887.3800 • *fac.* 215.887.3293 • desiree@ajaandalex.com

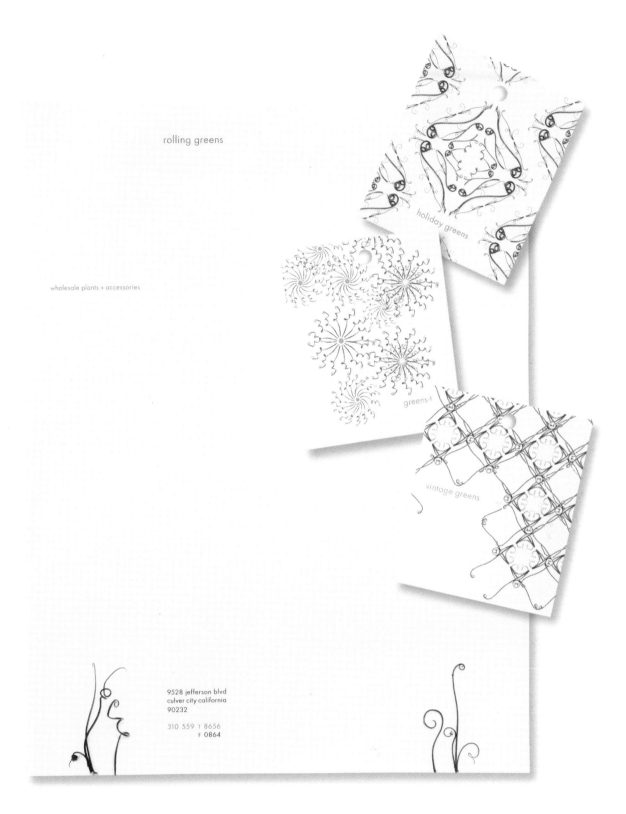

rolling greens

wholesale plants + accessories

holiday greens

greens-t

vintage greens

9528 jefferson blvd
culver city california
90232

310 559 T 8656
F 0864

blackwood

studios

studios

james vlahogiannis   blackwood

> 65 Blackwood Street Yarraville 3013 > PO BOX 135 Yarraville 3013
> T 03 9687 2345 > F 03 9687 4145 > M 0418 33 88 00
> E james@bwstudios.com.au > www.bwstudios.com.au

blackwood   studios

> Blackwood Studios Pty Ltd ABN 13 069 935 262
> 65 Blackwood Street Yarraville 3013 > PO BOX 135 Yarraville 3013
> T 03 9687 8818 > F 03 9687 4145 > M 0418 33 88 00
> E office@bwstudios.com.au > www.bwstudios.com.au

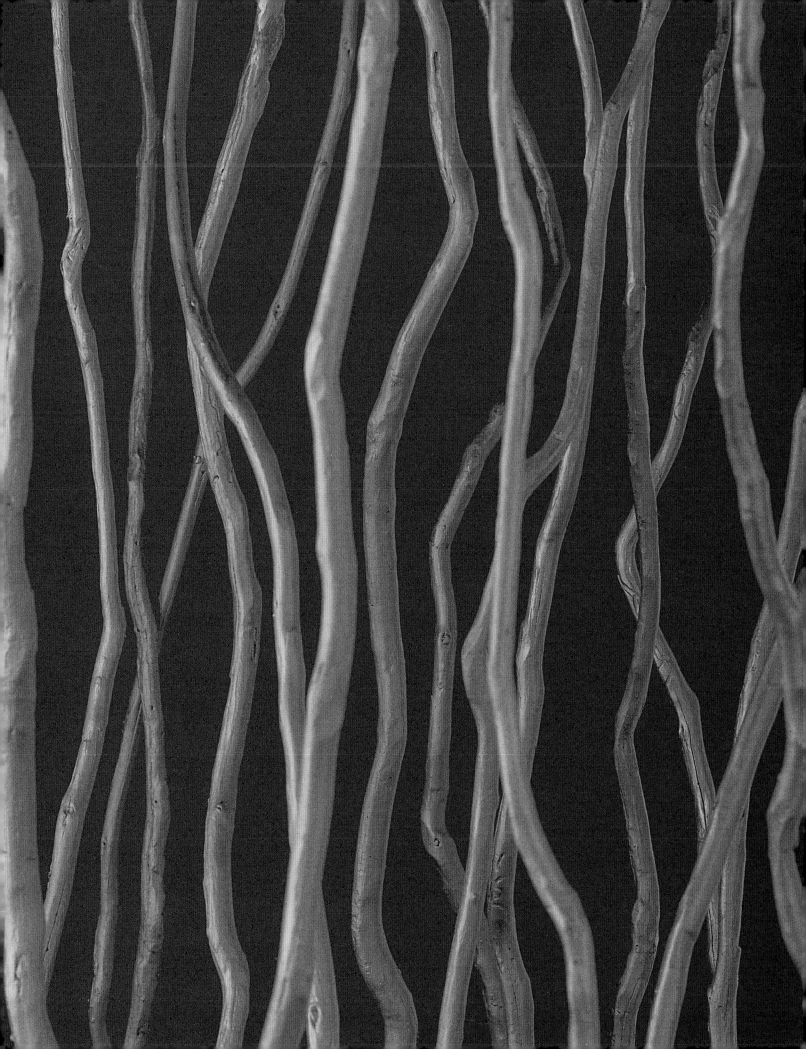

Wit and Whimsy: Intelligence, humor, double entendre, and folly. With winks and nods, these works elicited in us some visceral response that still lingers in our visual and intellectual memory. From esoteric homage to downright goofiness, we include here a selection of work that made us smile.

disgruntled

LEWIS COMMUNICATIONS—NASHVILLE | ART DIRECTOR ROBERT FROEDGE | CLIENT CAREER ENTERTAINMENT T.V.
FACING PAGE, TOP | WATTS DESIGN | DESIGNER PETER WATTS | CLIENT VICKI FREEMAN
FACING PAGE, BOTTOM | WATTS DESIGN | DESIGNER PETER WATTS | CLIENT TOM FREEMAN

Vicki Freeman
bean counter

T.G. Freeman & Associates ~ Accounting Services
24 Wallis Avenue, East Ivanhoe, Victoria, 3079
p 03 9499 2834 *f* 03 9499 8455 *e* tgfree@netlink.com.au

Vicki Freeman
bean counter

T.G. Freeman & Associates
ABN 29 004 494 580
Accounting Services
24 Wallis Avenue
East Ivanhoe 3079
p 03 9499 2834
f 03 9499 8455
e tgfree@netlink.com.au

Tom Freeman
underwater surveyor

T.G. Freeman & Associates
24 Wallis Avenue, East Ivanhoe, Victoria, 3079
p 0428 379 378 *f* 03 9499 8455 *e* tgfree@netlink.com.au

Tom Freeman
underwater surveyor

T.G. Freeman & Associates
24 Wallis Avenue, East Ivanhoe, Victoria, 3079
p 0428 379 378 *f* 03 9499 8455 *e* tgfree@netlink.com.au

1

2

3

1   PUNCHCUT | ART DIRECTOR JARED BENSON | DESIGNERS JARED BENSON, KEN OLEWILER | CLIENT PRAEDURUS
2   KINETIC SINGAPORE | ART DIECTORS PANN LIM, ROY POH, LENG SOH | DESIGNER LENG SOH | CLIENT PULLING STRINGS
3   ALPHABET ARM DESIGN | ART DIRECTOR AARON BELYEA | DESIGNER RYAN FREASE | CLIENT GHETTO ABNORM MUSIC

STUDIO A | ART DIRECTORS ARMANDO ANDRADE, VERÓNICA MAJLUF
DESIGNERS CLAUDIA JENSSEN, WALTER GUARDIA, ANA CECILIA PAZOS | CLIENT MAGENTA AIR

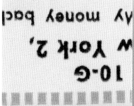
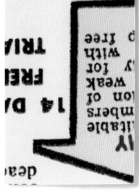

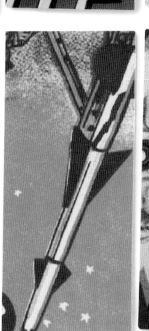

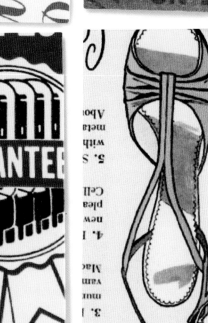

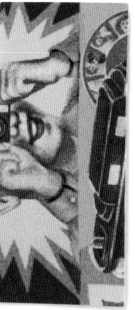

julie keenan, creative director

circle k studio

300 brannan street suite no. 308
san francisco california 94107
tel 415 243 0606 fax 415 243 0609
julie@circlekstudio.com

ALPHABET ARM DESIGN | ART DIRECTOR **AARON BELYEA** | DESIGNER **RYAN FREASE** | CLIENT **G2G MANAGEMENT/GARY GERSH**

1

2

SAMURAI GUPPY

YOUR TROPICAL FISH EXPERTS

3

1   UP DESIGN BUREAU | DESIGNER CHRIS PARKS | CLIENT JOSH CHRISTY
2   GLITSCHKA STUDIOS | DESIGNER VON R. GLITSCHKA | CLIENT SAMURAI GUPPY
3   UP DESIGN BUREAU | DESIGNER CHRIS PARKS | CLIENT MITCH WILLIS

BIG LAWN FILMS

1207 4TH STREET 5TH FLOOR PENTHOUSE 2 SANTA MONICA, CA 90401 **T 310.451 4148** F 310.451 8822
www.biglawnfilms.com

BIG LAWN FILMS

PH.D | ART DIRECTOR **CLIVE PIERCY** | DESIGNERS **CLIVE PIERCY, JOHN HUGHES** | CLIENT **BIG LAWN FILMS**

Golfing Society of the **Printing Industries Association of Australia** (Victorian Region)

PO Box 4203 Frankston Heights 3199 ℘ **03 9764 1445** ƒ **03 9764 1446** ℮ **bcasey@avongraphics.com.au**

WATTS DESIGN | DESIGNER **PETER WATTS** | CLIENT **PIAGS**

1

GPSS

2

3

1   SPARC, INC. | DESIGNER RICHARD CASSIS | CLIENT GOLF PRO SHOP SUPPLY
2   SABET BRANDS | DESIGNER ALI SABET | CLIENT AGILE HEALTH SERVICES
3   TURNER DUCKWORTH | ART DIRECTORS DAVID TURNER, BRUCE DUCKWORTH | DESIGNER SHAWN ROSENBERGER | CLIENT GREENBERG
     FACING PAGE | TANAGRAM PARTNERS | DESIGNER LANCE RUTTER | CLIENT TRIPLE TREE CAPITAL

TRIPLE TREE
CAPITAL

TRIPLE TREE
CAPITAL

333 NORTH MICHIGAN AVENUE, SUITE 2200, CHICAGO, ILLINOIS 60601

333 NORTH MICHIGAN AVENUE, SUITE 2200 • CHICAGO, ILLINOIS 60601 • T: 312.458.1406 • F: 312.458.0072 • WWW.TRIPLETREECAPITAL.COM

1

riocoffee

2

3

1 VOICE | ART DIRECTOR **ANTHONY DELEO** | DESIGNERS **ANTHONY DELEO, SCOTT CARSLAKE** | CLIENT **RIO COFFEE**
2 **METHOD ART & DESIGN** | DESIGNER **TRAVIS BROWN** | CLIENT **RICHMOND RACEWAY**
3 **METHOD ART & DESIGN** | DESIGNER **TRAVIS BROWN** | CLIENT **MOKAS**

1

↑ elevator

2

STORAGE

3

1   ELEVATOR | DESIGNER **TONY ADAMIC** | CLIENT **ELEVATOR**
2   **STUDIO SONSOLES LLORENS** | DESIGNER **STUDIO SONSOLES LLORENS** | CLIENT **STORAGE**
3   **GEYRHALTER DESIGN** | DESIGNER **FABIAN GEYRHALTER** | CLIENT **BABY YAGA**

1

HAIR

2

1   CIRCO DE BAKUZA | DESIGNER THOMAS CSANO | CLIENT JEAN VELUT
2   METHOD ART & DESIGN | DESIGNER TRAVIS BROWN | CLIENT CHRISTY PETERS

1

space

2

stealth

3

fuse

4

pottymouth

1   RED HERRING DESIGN | DESIGNER ANDREA SEPIC | CLIENT GRAY CAT RECORDS
2   RICOCHET CREATIVE THINKING | DESIGNER STEVE ZELLE | CLIENT STEALTH SECURITY
3   LISKA + ASSOCIATES | ART DIRECTOR STEVE LISKA | DESIGNER BRIAN GRAZIANO | CLIENT FUSE RESTAURANT
4   86 THE ONIONS | DESIGNER MARK SLOAN | CLIENT POTTYMOUTH

1

citrique

2

3

1   CINCO DE MAYO DESIGN | ART DIRECTOR **MAURICIO ALANIS** | DESIGNER **MAURICIO ALANIS, NOE FIGUEROA** | CLIENT **CRITIQUE**
2   **SIMON & GOETZ DESIGN** | ART DIRECTORS **PIA KEMPTER, RÜDIGER GOETZ** | DESIGNERS **GERRIT HINKELBEIN, PIA KEMPTER, RÜDIGER GOETZ** | CLIENT **ZDF**
3   **RED DOG DESIGN CONSULTANTS** | DESIGNER **MARY DOHERTY** | CLIENT **GIRAFFE CHILDCARE & EARLY LEARNING CENTRES**

1

2

3

4

1   GLITSCHKA STUDIOS | DESIGNER VON R. GLITSCHKA | CLIENT BLOGINTOSH.COM
2   PAVONE | DESIGNER ROBINSON SMITH | CLIENT DAYBREAK CHURCH
3   DESIGNSKI LLC | ART DIRECTOR DENNY KREGER | DESIGNERS CHRIS SNIEGOWSKI, DENNY KREGER | CLIENT CRUISEDIRECTOR.COM
4   FORM | ART DIRECTORS PAUL WEST, PAULA BENSON | DESIGNERS PAUL WEST, NICK HARD | CLIENT BRITISH SNOW & SKI FEDERATION

SAGMEISTER INC. | ART DIRECTOR STEFAN SAGMEISTER | DESIGNER MATTHIAS ERNSTBERGER | CLIENT VOLKSSCHULE

1

2

3

4

1 BONDEPUS DESIGN | ART DIRECTOR AMY BOND | DESIGNER GARY EPIS | CLIENT BARBAGELATA CONSTRUCTION
2 IRIDIUM | ART DIRECTORS JEAN-LUC DENAT, MARIO L'ÉCUYER | DESIGNERS MARIO L'ÉCUYER, ETIENNE BESSETTE | CLIENT TETHERCAM SYSTEMS
3 TREIBSTOFF WERBUNG | DESIGNERS THOMAS BIELICKI, BORIS KOCH | CLIENT TREIBSTOFF WERBUNG
4 SUSSNER DESIGN COMPANY | ART DIRECTOR DEREK SUSSNER | DESIGNER RYAN CARLSON | CLIENT AIGA, MINNESOTA

1

2

3

1   ALTERPOP | ART DIRECTOR DOROTHY REMINGTON | DESIGNER CHRISTOPHER SIMMONS | CLIENT PASTABILITIES
2   ENTERPRISE IG | DESIGNER BEVERLY FIELD | CLIENT SOUTH AFRICAN PREMIUM WINES
3   DAMION HICKMAN DESIGN | ART DIRECTOR DAMION HICKMAN | DESIGNER LEIGHTON HUBBELL | CLIENT SOAP BOX BATH & BODY

1

2

3

4

1   SABET BRANDS | DESIGNER ALI SABET | CLIENT STITCH BUNNY
2   VERLANDER DESIGN | DESIGNER MARK VERLANDER | CLIENT BASSET CLOTHING COMPANY
3   BE.DESIGN | ART DIRECTORS WILL BURKE, ERIC READ | DESIGNERS ERIC READ, YUSUKE ASAKA, CORALIE RUSSO | CLIENT DIGISCENTS
4   LLOYDS GRAPHIC DESIGN LTD | DESIGNER ALEXANDER LLOYD | CLIENT LAMBORGANIC

1

2

3

1   GRETEMAN GROUP | DESIGNER JAMES STRANGE | CLIENT KANSAS HUMANE SOCIETY
2   GARDNER DESIGN | ART DIRECTOR BILL GARDNER | DESIGNER LUKE BOTT | CLIENT STACK SHACK
3   UP DESIGN BUREAU | DESIGNER CHRIS PARKS | CLIENT ALAN MAIRS

BRIGHT NIGHT USA 6300 Merril Creek Parkway, Suite A-400, Everett, WA, USA 98203
P_425 398 4199 F_425 398 4177 info@brightnightusa.com

www.cyclite.com www.stridelite.com

Our products are designed by people who are out there enjoying an active life, just like you. And we know that safety and reliability are important when the light is low and you are miles from nowhere. Every CycLite™ and StrideLite® product features 24-micron-thin Electroluminescent Lamps that are completely flexible, virtually weightless and highly durable. This high-intensity light and 3M™ reflective material offer unparalleled, 360° visibility from up to 1/2 mile. Though powerful, the blue strobe-lite incorporates an innovative low-power platform that allows 2 "AAA" batteries to last 200+ hours. But safety doesn't have to be boring; all CycLite™ and StrideLite® products are functional fashion. After all, it's not just about being seen in the dark, it's about "being seen" out there.

YOU CAN RUN BUT YOU CAN'T HIDE

CycLite™ **StrideLite®**

→ **SAFETY NOTICE**
STROBE-LITE SAFETY GEAR FOR RUNNERS + CYCLISTS

1

2

3

FACING PAGE | **SUBPLOT DESIGN INC.** | DESIGNERS **MATTHEW CLARK, ROY WHITE** | CLIENT **BRIGHT NIGHT USA**

1 **Y & R** | ART DIRECTOR **SCOTT LARSON** | DESIGNER **CHRIS ROONEY** | CLIENT **SAN FRANCISCO FILM SOCIETY**

2 **DOSSIERCREATIVE INC.** | ART DIRECTOR **DON CHISHOLM** | DESIGNER **PATRICK SMITH** | CLIENT **WHITE SPOT RESTAURANT**

3 **A-BOMBE** | DESIGNER **SJKG** | CLIENT **FREAKLAB**

PING-PONG DESIGN | DESIGNER PING-PONG DESIGN | CLIENT BBK DOOR VRIENDSCHAP STERKER / BERT RORIJE

CALDWELL
— ZOO —

1   EVENSON DESIGN GROUP | ART DIRECTOR STAN EVENSON | DESIGNER MARK SOJKA | CLIENT ANGEL CITY FITNESS
2   HARRAINCO SKIPP HERRAINCO | ART DIRECTOR RAY HRYNKOW | DESIGNER DYLAN STANIUL | CLIENT GRADY WINE MARKETING
3   SULLIVANPERKINS | ART DIRECTOR ROB WILSON | DESIGNER JARROD HOLT | CLIENT CALDWELL ZOO

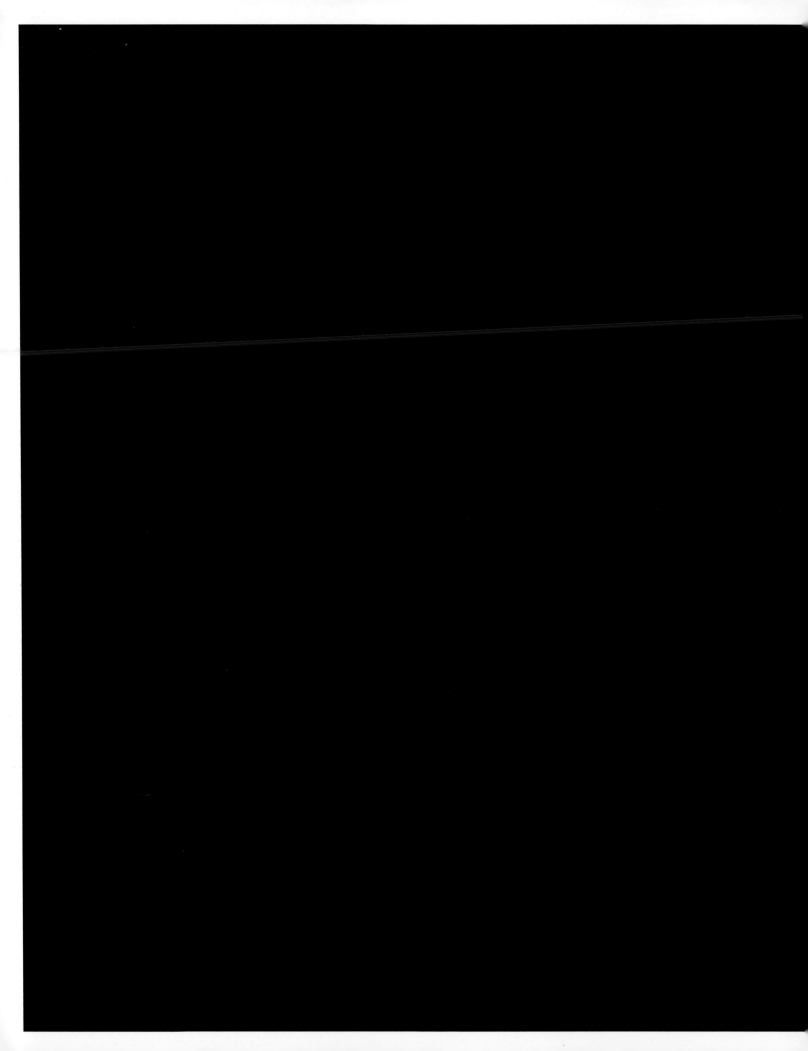

Simplicity: The confidence to be the very least. Whether in concept or form, the following were selected for the succinctness of their expression. Never more than they need to be, these works embody the pithy spirit of minimalism— even the seemingly complex are underpinned by the virtue of their simplicity.

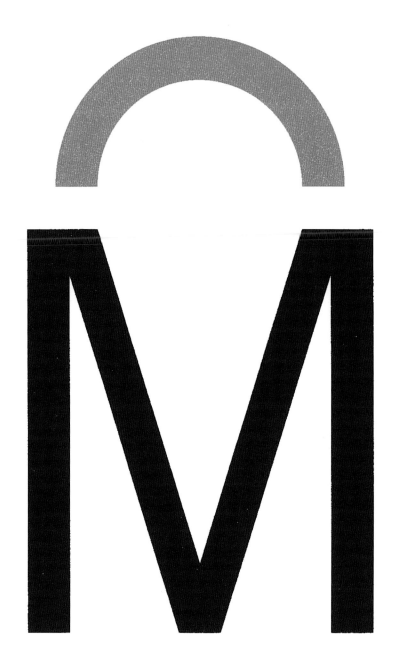

PENTAGRAM DESIGN/SF | ART DIRECTOR **BRIAN JACOBS** | DESIGNER **ROB DUNCAN** | CLIENT **CAFÉ MIA**

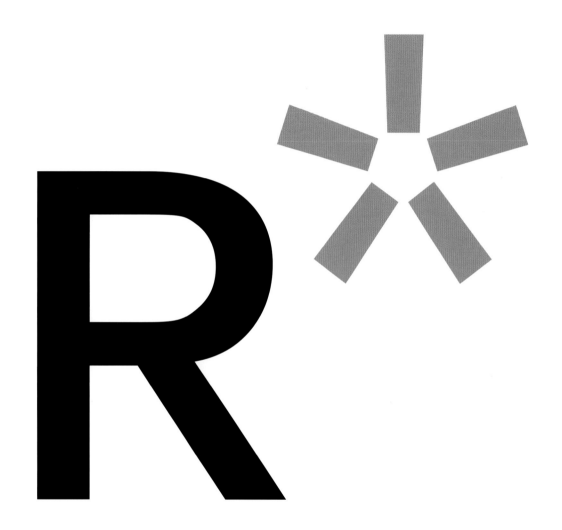

BOY + GIRL DESIGN | DESIGNER **TODD VERLANDER** | CLIENT **JON RADEL PHOTOGRAPHY**

wemakedesign VVVA

nicola dillon
creative design consultant

2 janeville, off st. kevins parade, dublin 8
telephone + 353 1 473 8498
mobile + 353 87 643 2829
email nik@wemakedesign.com
website www.wemakedesign.com

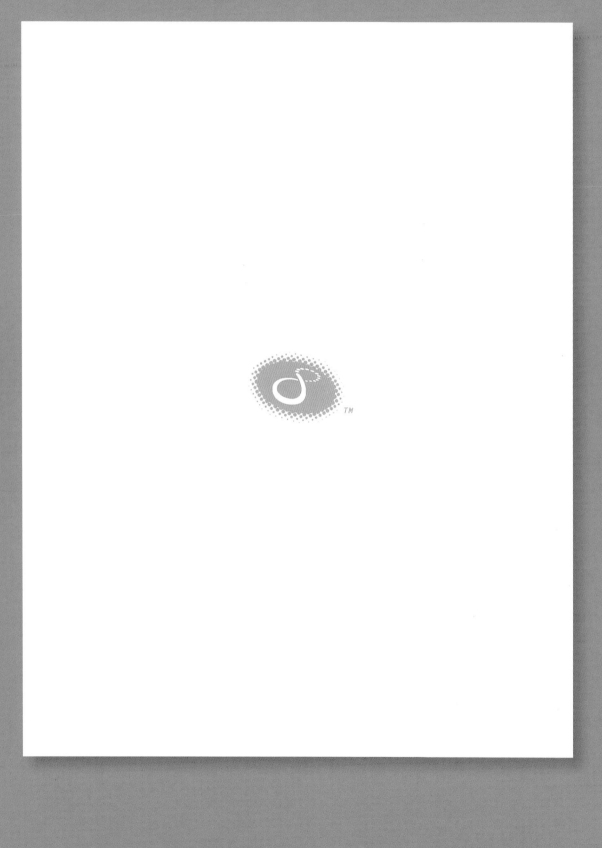

PREVIOUS SPREAD, LEFT | **WEMAKE DESIGN** | ART DIRECTOR **NIK DILLON** | DESIGNERS **NIK DILLON, ADAM GALLACHER** | CLIENT **WEMAKE DESIGN**
PREVIOUS SPREAD, RIGHT | **DESIGN INFINITUM** | DESIGNER **JAMES A. SMITH** | CLIENT **DESIGN INFINITUM**
PH. D. | ART DIRECTORS **CLIVE PIERCY, MICHAEL HODGSON** | DESIGNERS **CLIVE PIERCY, CAROL KONO, MICHAEL HODGSON** | CLIENT **DNA**

Mortgage**Selection**Services

Mortgage Selection Services Pty Ltd
ABN 96 080 116 454
Level 1, 150 Albert Road
South Melbourne 3205 Victoria
Telephone 03 9686 3322
Facsimile 03 9686 3518
www.mortgagess.com.au

Member MIAA
Melbourne
Sydney

Marina Lindner

Mortgage**Selection**Services
Member MIAA

OCTAVO DESIGN | ART DIRECTOR **GARY DOMONEY** | CLIENT **MORTGAGE SELECTION SERVICES**

Matsuzaki, Yumi [yümi məsuzaki]
n. A young designer who wants to make
the world a better place through her designs.
229West 109thSt Apt#52 New York, NY 10025
Tel 212 961 0363 Email aur3tx@hotmail.com

eliminating racism empowering women
ywca

LANDOR ASSOCIATES | ART DIRECTOR MARGARET YOUNGBLOOD | DESIGNERS KISITINA WONG, JOHN LEDWITH | CLIENT YWCA

design

intelligent

sweet pea gourmet

Leslie Owen
personal chef

1005 Lindridge Dr. NE
Atlanta, GA 30324
E leslie@sweetpeagourmet.com
P 404.232.5663   F 404.816.1411

1005 Lindridge Dr. NE   Atlanta, GA 30324   P (404) 232.5663   F (404) 816.1411   W sweetpeagourmet.com

SKY DESIGN | ART DIRECTOR **W. TODD VAUGHT** | DESIGNER **W. TODD VAUGHT** | CLIENT **SWEET PEA GOURMET**

DAVE BRADLEY PHOTOGRAPHY

840 Summer Street Boston MA 02127 USA Tel: 617.268.6644 Fax: 617.268.3025 Web: davebradleyphoto.com

PRESENT PAGE | **BLACKCOFFEE®** | ART DIRECTOR **MARK GALLAGHER** | DESIGNER **LAURA SAVARD** | CLIENT **DAVE BRADLEY PHOTOGRAPHY**
1   **VERLANDER DESIGN** | DESIGNER **MARK VERLANDER** | CLIENT **SUPPOSE**
2   **ELLEN GOULD** | CLIENT **DIESEL, A BOOKSTORE**
3   **BRAIN MAGNET** | CLIENT **BRAIN MAGNET**

1

2

3

Brain Magnet

claus semerak Kunsthistoriker Freier Journalist
corneliusstraße 23   80469 münchen   t 089 - 202 45 151   f 089 - 202 45 152   m 0163 - 202 45 15
www.claussemerak.de   info@claussemerak.de

claus semerak Kunsthistoriker Freier Journalist
corneliusstraße 23   80469 münchen
t 089 - 202 45 151   f 089 - 202 45 152   m 0163 - 202 45 15
www.claussemerak.de   info@claussemerak.de

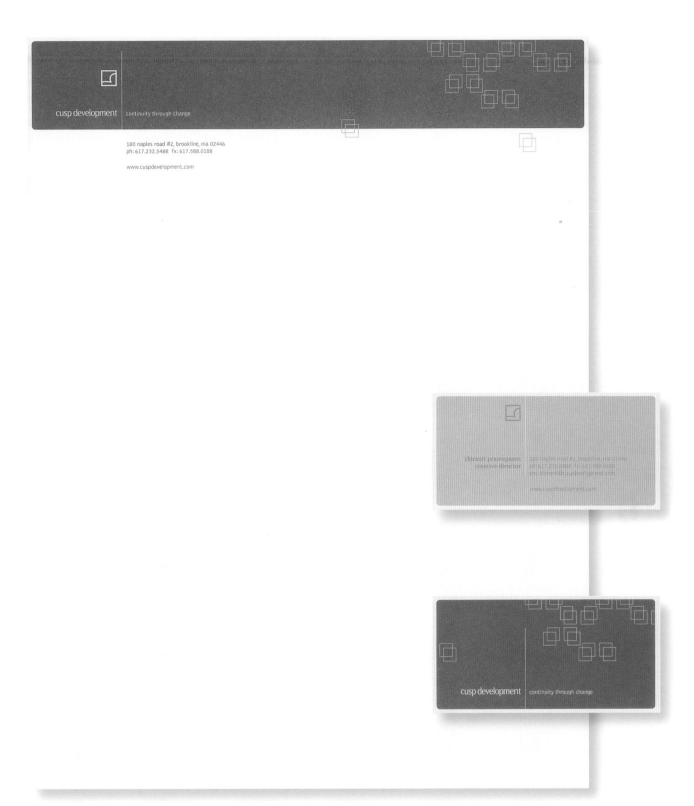

FACING PAGE | **MILCH DESIGN** | ART DIRECTOR **FRIEDEL PATZAK** | DESIGNER **INA WINDHORST** | CLIENT **CLAUS SEMERAK**
CUSP DESIGN | DESIGNER **CHIRANIT PRATEEPASEN** | CLIENT **CUSP DEVELOPMENT**

1

ÍV

cosmeceuticals

2

BRANDOCTOR✛

3

andisa

1   DOSSIERCREATIVE INC. | ART DIRECTOR DON CHISHOLM | DESIGNER EENA KIM | CLIENT AG HAIR COSMETICS, INC.
2   BRUKETA & ZINIC | DESIGNER SINISA SUDAR | CLIENT BRANDOCTOR
3   ENTERPRISE IG | DESIGNER BEVERLEY FIELD | CLIENT ANDISA CAPITAL

DOSSIERCREATIVE INC. | ART DIRECTOR DON CHISHOLM | DESIGNER EENA KIM | CLIENT AG HAIR COSMETICS, INC.

1

2

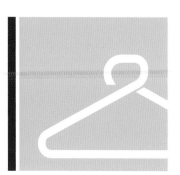

3

1   ENTERPRISE IG | ART DIRECTOR **IAAN BEKKER** | DESIGNER **COLLETTE WASIELEWSKI** | CLIENT **GUARANTY TRUST BANK**
2   BUROCRATIK | DESIGNERS **FILIPE CAVACO JORGE, ADRIANO ESTEVES** | CLIENT **KASALTA - INDÚSTRIA DE MOBILIÁRIO, LDA.**
3   TALISMAN INTERACTIVE | DESIGNER **MICHAEL MCDONALD** | CLIENT **OWEN PATRICK GALLERY**

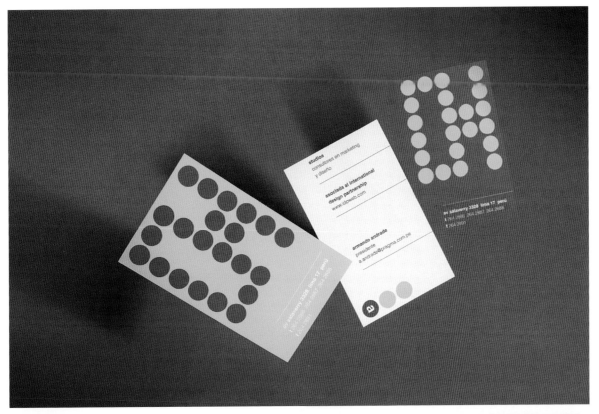

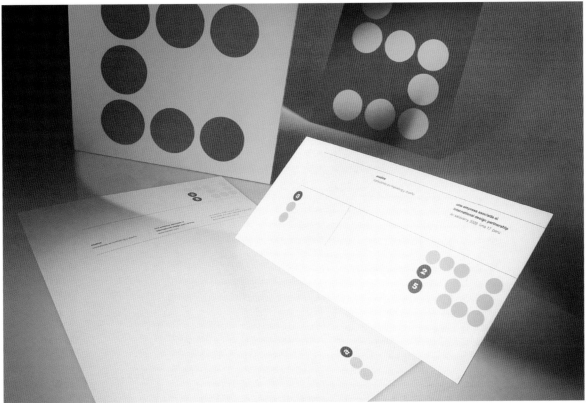

nina DaviD
kommunikationsdesign

nina DaviD
kommunikationsdesign

Eisenstraße 31 . 40227 Düsseldorf
Fon 0211.7 333 290 Fax 0211.7 952 441
Handy 0178.888 66 00

mail@ninadavid.de

Eisenstraße 31 . 40227 Düsseldorf
Fon 0211.7 333 290 Fax 0211.7 952 441
mail@ninadavid.de

1

2

3

FACING PAGE | NINA DAVID KOMMUNIKATIONSDESIGN | DESIGNER NINA DAVID | CLIENT NINA DAVID KOMMUNIKATIONSDESIGN
1   MONDERER DESIGN | ART DIRECTOR STEWART MONDERER | DESIGNERS STEWART MONDERER, TR COFFEY | CLIENT WIND DEVELOPMENT, LTD.
2   BAM AGENCY | ART DIRECTOR RICK YORK | DESIGNER VON R. GLITSCHKA | CLIENT VIP INDUSTRIES
3   JAGER GROUP | ART DIRECTORS ROB JACKSON, ANDY FILIUS | DESIGNER GREY PALAZOLLO | CLIENT FAST KAT FERRY SERVICES

John J. Guarracino, DDS

John J. Guarracino, DDS

Medical and Executive Center ○ 1023 Route 146
Clifton Park, NY 12065
ph: 518.383.9257 ○ f: 518.383.9235

Medical and Executive Center ○ 1023 Route 146 ○ Clifton Park, NY 12065
ph: 518.383.9257 ○ f: 518.383.9235

TEMALIDESIGN | DESIGNER **TERRI ROSEN** | CLIENT **JOHN J. GUARRACINO, DDS**

LAW OFFICE VUKINA
Prilaz Gjure Deželića 30, 10000 Zagreb, Croatia
Tel. + (3851) 4874 970, Fax + (3851) 4874 971
E-mail: info@vukina.hr

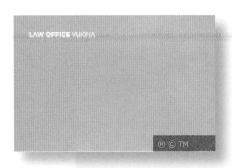

BRUKETA & ZINIC | DESIGNER **IGOR MANASTERIOTTI** | CLIENT **LAW OFFICE VUKINA**
FACING PAGE | **IRIDIUM** | DESIGNER **MARIO L'ÉCUYER** | CLIENT **CALLAGHAN POTTER LETELLIER**

CPL

Callaghan Potter Letellier
Facility Planners

Jim Potter B.E.S. (Architecture)

211–2141 Thurston Drive
Ottawa Ontario K1G 6C9
T 613-739-3699
F 613-739-3965
E jim@cpldesign.on.ca

Callaghan Potter Letellier
Design Consultants Inc.

211–2141 Thurston Drive Ottawa Ontario K1G 6C9
T 613-739-3699   F 613-739-3965   E info@cpldesign.on.ca

CPL

elgato

elgato systems GmbH   Nymphenburger Str. 86   D-80636 München   Germany

elgato

Freddie Geier
CEO

freddie@elgato.com

elgato systems GmbH   T +49 (0)89 143339-0   HypoVereinsbank AG München   Amtsgericht München   Geschäftsführer
Nymphenburger Str. 86   F +49 (0)89 143339-99   BLZ 700 202 70, Kto 48 2454 20   HRB 108591   Dr. Markus Fest
D-80636 München   www.elgato.com   StNr 810/254 26   UStID DE169235722   Freddie Geier

	USA	AUSTRALIA
LOCATION	PO Box 2441 La Jolla, CA 92038-2441 USA	17 Killara St. Currumbin Waters Queensland, Australia 4223
PHONE	858 724 0818	+61 7 5534 8269
FACSIMILE	858 724 0819	+61 7 5534 8652
WEB	**www.metcorpusa.com**	

MET | CORPORATION

WORLD PRODUCT TRADERS

FACING PAGE | **MILCH DESIGN** | DESIGNER **FRIEDEL PATZAK** | CLIENT **ELGATO**
TYPE G | DESIGNER **MIKE NELSON** | CLIENT **MET CORPORATION**

❧ OLD EUROPE ❧
Legal Translation Services

John P. McAlonan, Esq.
Principal

❧ OLD EUROPE ❧
Translation Services for the Legal Profession

DEUTSCH   FRANÇAIS   AMERICAN ENGLISH

Principal
John P. McAlonan, Esq.

315 Bleecker St, Suite 286   T/F 212 243 1856
New York, NY 10014   E *info@oldeuropetranslation.com*

oldeuropetranslation.com

315 Bleecker St, Suite 286   New York, NY 10014   tel/fax 212 243 1856   info@oldeuropetranslation.com   oldeuropetranslation.com

1

2

FACING PAGE | VINEGAR HILL PRINTERS, LLC | DESIGNER AMELIA GROHMAN | CLIENT OLD EUROPE LEGAL TRANSLATION SERVICES
1   GINGERBEE CREATIVE | DESIGNER GINGER KNAFF | CLIENT MOOSE MAGOO'S
2   DOTZERO DESIGN | DESIGNERS JON WIPPICH, KAREN WIPPICH | CLIENT PERSIMMON CONSTRUCTION LLC

fabulous

Fabulous Films Inc.

3301 Fernwood Avenue, Silverlake,
Los Angeles, CA 90039, USA.
Telephone: +1 323 663 0929.
Fax: +1 323 663 0926.

Fabulous Films Ltd.

26 Loftus Road, London, W12 7EN, UK.
Telephone: +44 (0)208 743 4377.
Fax: +44 (0)208 743 4342.

Web: www.fabulousfilms.co.uk   Email: info@fabulousfilms.co.uk

1

evo

2

3

P / N W H E E L ™

FACING PAGE | **FORM** | ART DIRECTOR **PAUL WEST** | DESIGNERS **PAUL WEST, NICK HARD** | CLIENT **FABULOUS FILMS**
1   **HERRAINCO SKIPP HERRAINCO** | ART DIRECTOR **CASEY HRYNKOW** | DESIGNER **KIRSTEN GRAVKIN** | CLIENT **EVO PERSONAL & BUSINESS DEVELOPMENT COACHING**
2   **SIMON & GOETZ DESIGN** | ART DIRECTORS **RÜDIGER GOETZ, ANNE MÜLDER** | DESIGNERS **ANNE MÜLDER, ANTON STEPANCHUK** | CLIENT **HS GENION**
3   **TALISMAN INTERACTIVE** | DESIGNER **MICHAEL MCDONALD** | CLIENT **PINWHEEL**

1

2

3

BERGAMOT CAFE

1   METHOD ART + DESIGN | DESIGNER TRAVIS BROWN | CLIENT TRUMPET CARDS
2   RICK JOHNSON & COMPANY | CREATIVE DIRECTOR SAM MACLAY | DESIGNER TIM MCGRATH | CLIENT MATTEUCCI CONSTRUCTION
3   PH.D | ART DIRECTORS MICHAEL HODGSON, CLIVE PIERCY | DESIGNER MICHAEL HODGSON | CLIENT BERGAMOT CAFÉ

SALVA O'RENICK | DESIGNER **MICHAEL PAOLETTI** | CLIENT **SUGAR CREEK FAIR & FESTIVAL BOARD**
NEXT SPREAD, LEFT | **CHEN DESIGN ASSOCIATES** | ART DIRECTOR **JOSHUA C. CHEN** | DESIGNER **MAX SPECTOR** | CLIENT **QUALITY OF LIFE**
NEXT SPREAD, RIGHT | **LLOYDS GRAPHIC DESIGN LTD.** | DESIGNER **ALEXANDER LLOYD** | CLIENT **WINE BOTTLERS MARLBOROUGH**

QUALITY OF LIFE

WHERE DO YOU DRAW THE LINE?

www.qualityoflife-themovie.com

wine**bottlers**
marlborough ltd

wine, sealed, delivered

Wine Bottlers Marlborough Ltd

Cloudy Bay Business Park
SH1, PO Box 1176, Blenheim
New Zealand

Tel: +64 3 577 5350
Fax: +64 3 577 5350
Email: info@winebottlers.co.nz

1

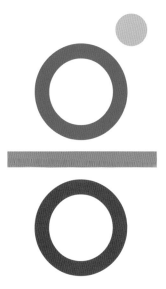

2

DAVIES ASSOCIATES | ART DIRECTOR **CATHY DAVIES** | DESIGNER **PAUL HERSHFIELD** | CLIENT **COX PAINT**

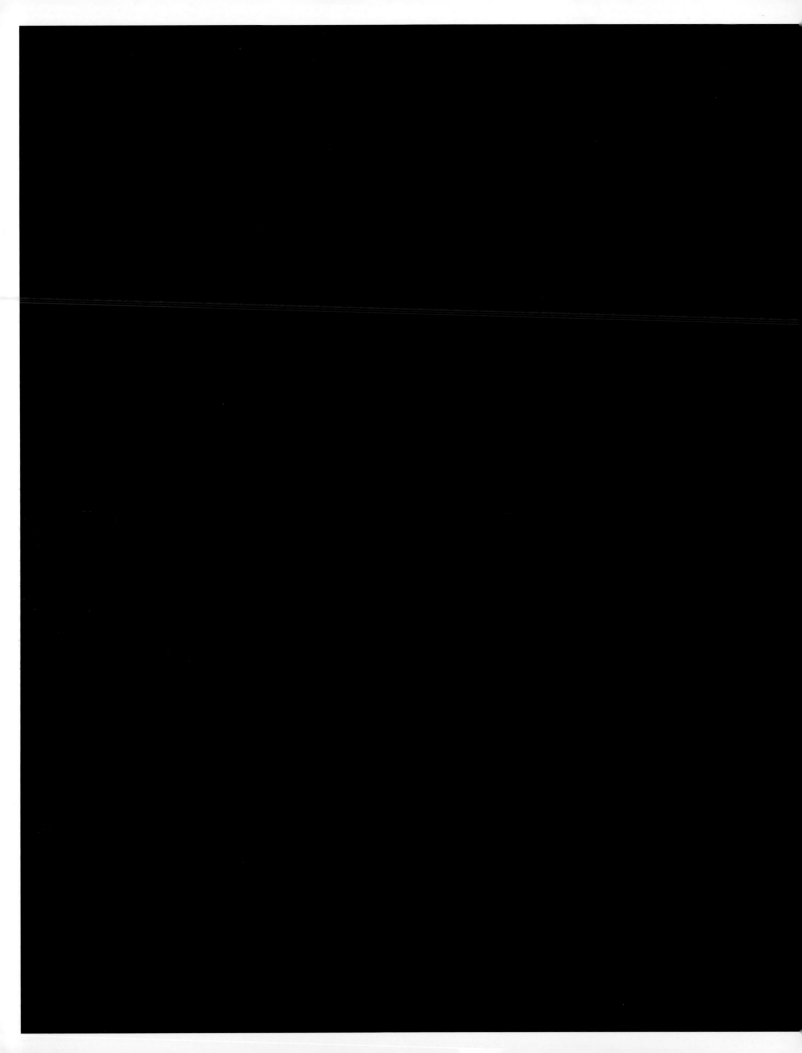

Subtlety: The smallest discernible difference. Through color, form, scale, or concept, these works exhibit the artful restraint of their creators. In each instance, we found finesse and nuance made the difference. Look closely—design is in the details.

The Riordon Design Group Inc.   131 George Street   TEL 905.339.0750
www.riordondesign.com   Oakville, ON L6J 3B9   FAX 905.339.0753

WOW! BRANDING | ART DIRECTOR **PERRY CHUA** | DESIGNERS **WILL JOHNSON, TARA RICE, JEFF SCHRAMM** | CLIENT **GLUMAC**

ISOTOPE 221

Christopher Cannon   info@isotope221.com

232 Washington Avenue   718.783.3092 *tel*
Fourth Floor   270.477.6850 *fax*
Brooklyn, NY 11205   www.isotope221.com

232 Washington Avenue   718.783.3092 *tel*   Annual reports, collateral, corporate identity, editorial design,
Fourth Floor   270.477.6850 *fax*   interactive presentations, packaging, product development,
Brooklyn, NY 11205   info@isotope221.com   website design: ISOTOPE 221 solves communications problems.

cherrydelosreyes

12611 Venice Boulevard
Los Angeles California
90066-3703   310 398 7404 fax 7406

cherrydelosreyes.com

PREVIOUS SPREAD, LEFT | **ISOTOPE 221** | DESIGNER **CHRISTOPHER CANNON** | CLIENT **ISOTOPE 221**
PREVIOUS SPREAD, RIGHT | **MERYL POLLEN DESIGN** | DESIGNER **MERYL POLLEN** | CLIENT **CHERRYDELOSREYES**
XMI DESIGN | ART DIRECTOR **DENIS KELLY** | DESIGNERS **NOELLE COOPER, DENIS KELLY** | CLIENT **XMI DESIGN**

2111 West Churchill, Suite 106

premonitionandmusic.com

Premonition Records

v.773.486.2333 f.773.486.2338

Chicago, Illinois 60647

HUTCHINSON ASSOCIATES, IND. | ART DIRECTOR JERRY HUTCHINSON | DESIGNERS AL BRANDTNER, JERRY HUTCHINSON | CLIENT PREMONITION RECORDS

MORTENSEN DESIGN INC. | ART DIRECTOR GORDON MORTENSEN | DESIGNER HELENA SEO | CLIENT MORTENSEN DESIGN INC.
FACING PAGE | TILKA DESIGN | ART DIRECTOR JANE TILKA | DESIGNER TILKA DESIGN | CLIENT WHITEBOX

WHITEBOX

3033 Excelsior Boulevard I Suite 300 I Minneapolis, MN 55416
612-253-6001 I *fax* 612-253-6151 I www.whiteboxadvisors.com

NOON

NOON | 592 UTAH STREET | SAN FRANCISCO | CALIFORNIA 94110
TELEPHONE (415)621-4922 | FACSIMILE (415)621-4966
www.designatnoon.com

www.designatnoon.com | TELEPHONE (415)621-4922 | FACSIMILE (415)621-4966 | 592 UTAH STREET | SAN FRANCISCO | CALIFORNIA 94110

merry
monk
design

1200 Washington Street, Studio 114
Boston, MA 01118 | Tel 617.698.5174

MERRYMONKDESIGN.COM

Inspiration   considers   the unexpected.
Reason   incorporates everything.
Imagination   creates   good fortune.

merry
monk
design

FACING PAGE | NOON | DESIGNER CINTHIA WEN | CLIENT NOON
CUSP DESIGN | DESIGNER CHIRANIT PRATEEPASEN | CLIENT MERRY MONK DESIGN

warehouse¹
www.wh1.com

7800 E. 12th Street
Kansas City, MO 64126

phone 816.483.6999
fax 816.231.7333

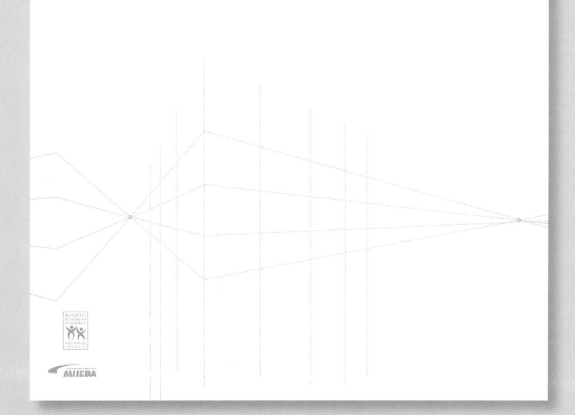

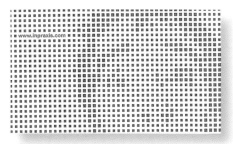

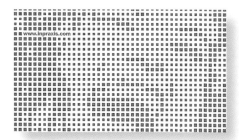

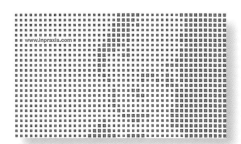

CAMPAIGN *for* THE FIELD MUSEUM

UNDERSTAND THE PAST
SHAPE THE FUTURE

The Field
Museum

Campaign Cabinet

Marshall B. Front
   Chairman, Capital Campaign
Judith S. Block
Robert W. Crawford, Jr.
Marshall Field
   Chairman, Board of Trustees
Ronald J. Gidwitz
Mellody Hobson
William C. Kunkler
John W. McCarter, Jr.
   President and CEO
Cary J. Malkin
Neil S. Novich
Richard Pigott
Adele S. Simmons
Miles D. White

1400 South Lake Shore Drive
Chicago, Illinois 60605-2496
(312) 665-7776 telephone
(312) 665-7778 fax
www.fieldmuseum.org

ADAMO LONDON

444

SARATOGA AVENUE, SUITE 2D
SANTA CLARA
CALIFORNIA 95050

FACSIMILE 408 241 7215
www.adamolondon.com

408 391 8421

nh@adamolondon.com

from the desk of
NADIM KHAN HASHIM

peterson ARCHitects 1126 folsom street, #3, san francisco, CALIFORNIA 94103 TELEPHONE 415.431.6600 FACSIMILE 415.431.9695

peterson ARCHitects

1126 folsom street, #3, san francisco, CALIFORNIA 94103

www.petersonarch.com

TELEPHONE 415.431.6600 FACSIMILE 415.431.9695

1126 folsom street, #3, san francisco, CALIFORNIA 94103

1126 folsom street, #3, san francisco, CALIFORNIA 94103

PREVIOUS SPREAD, LEFT | **COSTELLO COMMUNICATIONS** | DESIGNER **JAMES COSTELLO** | CLIENT **THE FIELD MUSEUM**
PREVIOUS SPREAD, RIGHT | **CHEN DESIGN** | ART DIRECTOR **JOSHUA C. CHEN** | DESIGNERS **JENNIFER TOLO, MAX SPECTOR** | CLIENT **ADAMO LONDON**
MENDE DESIGN | DESIGNER **JEREMY MENDE** | CLIENT **PETERSON ARCHITECTS**

NancyNimoy

www.nancynimoy.com nancy@nancynimoy.com
Helms Building | 8800 Venice Blvd Suite 215 | Culver City CA 90034
Studio: 310 558 8350   Cell: 310 351 9342   Fax: 310 558 8351

PH.D | DESIGNER **MICHAEL HODGSON** | CLIENT **NANCY NIMOY**

GARY TARDIFF

850 Summer Street
Boston Ma 02127
tel 617 464 4555
fax 617 464 4524
culinaryphoto.com

GARY TARDIFF

850 Summer Street
Boston Ma 02127
tel 617 464 4555
fax 617 464 4524
culinaryphoto.com

GARY TARDIFF

850 Summer Street
Boston Ma 02127
tel 617 464 4555
fax 617 464 4524
culinaryphoto.com

1

2

napa valley vintners

FACING PAGE | **BLACKCOFFEE®** | ART DIRECTOR **MARK GALLAGHER** | DESIGNER **LAURA SAVARD** | CLIENT **GARY TARDIFF PHOTOGRAPHY**
1   **GARDNER DESIGN** | ART DIRECTOR **BILL GARDNER** | DESIGNER **LUKE BOTT** | CLIENT **PLASTIC SURGERY CENTER**
2   **LANDOR ASSOCIATES** | ART DIRECTOR **NICOLAS APARICIO** | DESIGNERS **ANASTASIA LAKSMI, KISITINA WONG** | CLIENTS **NAPA VALLEY VINTNERS ASSOC.**

CAFÉ OPALINE

CAFÉ OPALINE
AT DAHESH MUSEUM OF ART
580 Madison Avenue New York, NY USA 10022
T 212.521.8155 F 212.521.8159
daheshmuseum.org

MORTENSEN DESIGN, INC. | ART DIRECTOR **GORDON MORTENSEN** | DESIGNER **ANN JORDAN**
CLIENT **CHRISTINE MORTENSEN RESIDENTIAL GARDEN DESIGN**

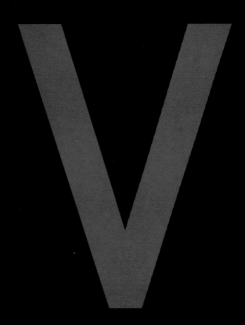

Virtuosity: a higher standard. In any group, there are leaders. The technical skill, originality, and authenticity of the following work represents a level of fluency and standard of excellence that merits special consideration. The ideas, forms, and functions expressed in these selections inspired in us a sense of awe, and a degree of envy.

1

2

3

1   VERLANDER DESIGN | DESIGNER MARK VERLANDER | CLIENT NATIONAL FOOTBALL LEAGUE
2   VERLANDER DESIGN | DESIGNER MARK VERLANDER | CLIENT NATIONAL FOOTBALL LEAGUE
3   VERLANDER DESIGN | DESIGNER MARK VERLANDER | CLIENT NATIONAL FOOTBALL LEAGUE

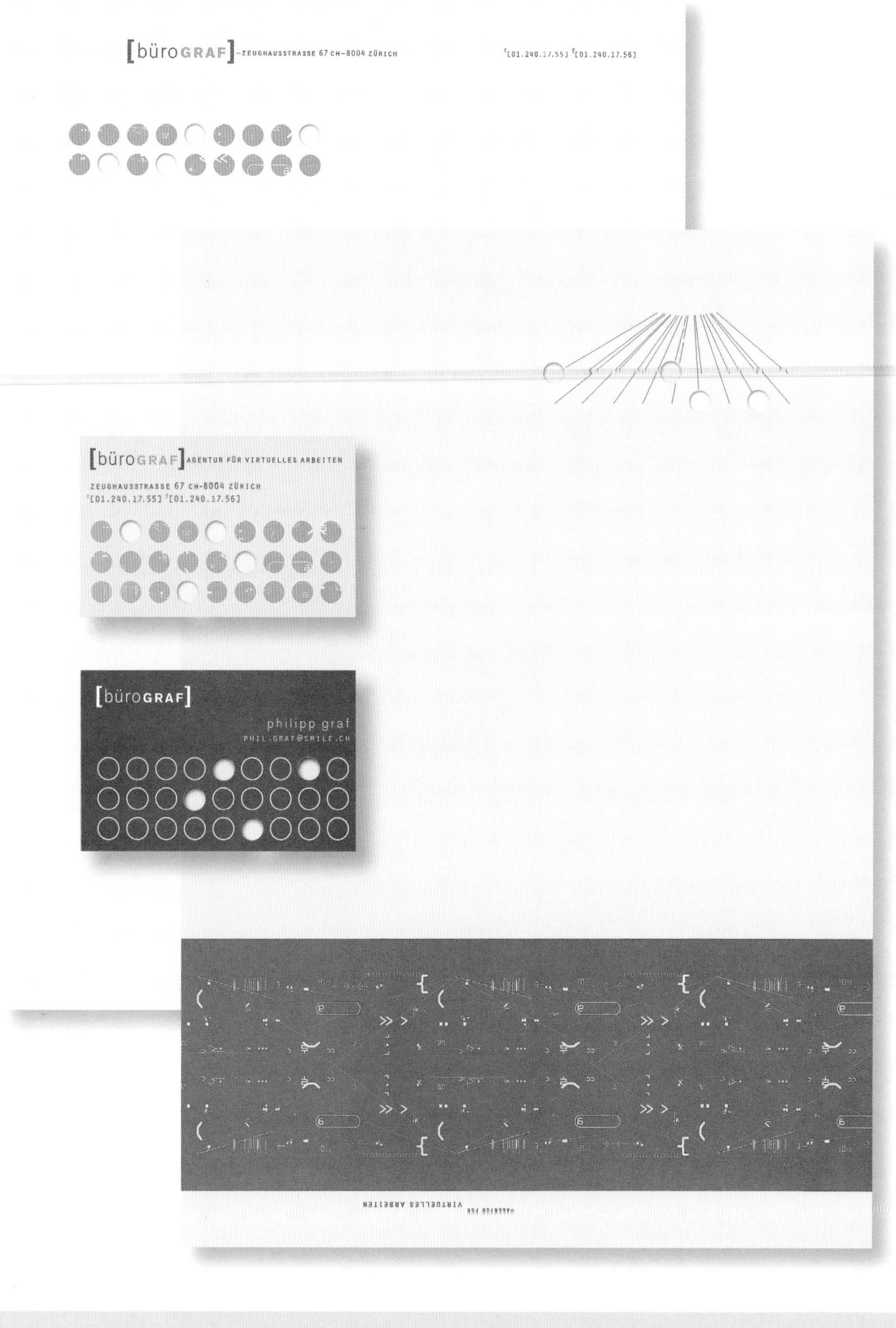

138

[büroGRAF]—ZEUGHAUSSTRASSE 67 CH—8004 ZÜRICH   [01.240.17.55] [01.240.17.56]

[büroGRAF] AGENTUR FÜR VIRTUELLES ARBEITEN

ZEUGHAUSSTRASSE 67 CH—8004 ZÜRICH
[01.240.17.55] [01.240.17.56]

[büroGRAF]

philipp graf
PHIL.GRAF@SMILE.CH

SAGMEISTER INC.

Stefan@Sagmeister.com
222 West 14th Street, Suite 15A
New York City, NY 10011
T 212·647 1789 F 212·647 1788
www.Sagmeister.com

STEFAN SAGMEISTER

SAGMEISTER, INC. | ART DIRECTOR **STEFAN SAGMEISTER** | DESIGNERS **MATTHIAS ERNSTBERGER, SARAH NOELLENHEIDT**
CLIENT **SAGMEISTER, INC.**

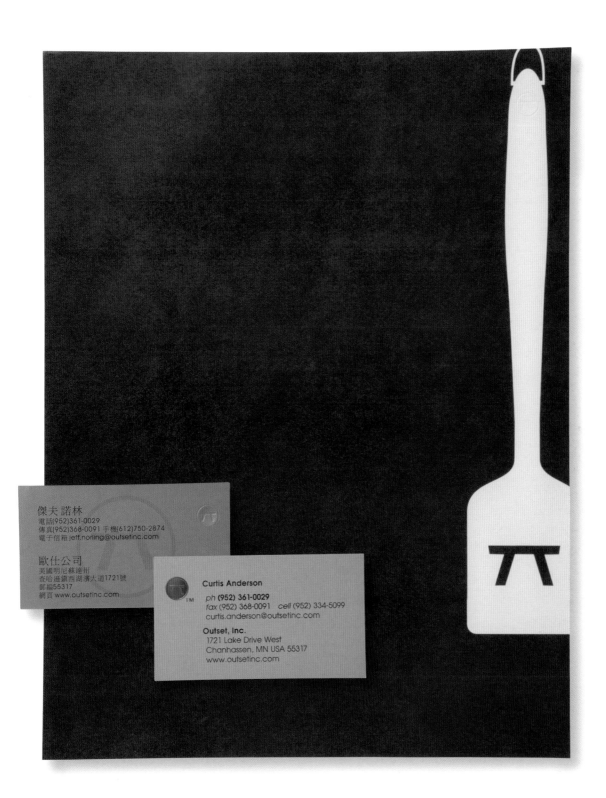

FACING PAGE | **MENDE DESIGN** | ART DIRECTOR **JEREMY MENDE** | DESIGNERS **JEREMY MENDE, MOLLY SKONIECZNY**
CLIENT **GLS LANDSCAPE ARCHITECTURE**
AKA CREATIVE | DESIGNER **AMY ANDERSON** | CLIENT **OUTSET, INC.**

WILLOUGHBY DESIGN GROUP | ART DIRECTOR **ANN WILLOUGHBY** | DESIGNER **LINDSAY LARRICKS** | CLIENT **KEVIN CARROLL**
FACING PAGE | **SALT BRANDING** | ART DIRECTOR **PAUL PARKIN** | DESIGNER **CESAR CHIN** | CLIENT **TRIBE.NET**

tribe.net
local connections

1

2

1   SULLIVANPERKINS | DESIGNER CHUCK JOHNSON | CLIENT YAVNEH ACADEMY
2   MANASTERIOTTI DESIGN STUDIO | DESIGNER IGOR MANASTERIOTTI | CLIENT CENTER FOR GENDER EQUALITY

1

2

1   RICK JOHNSON & COMPANY | ART DIRECTOR **SAM MACLAY** | DESIGNER **TIM MCGRATH** | CLIENT **OILSLICK IMPORTS**
2   **VERLANDER DESIGN** | DESIGNER **MARK VERLANDER** | CLIENT **PRIMA VINI**

TARTINE

ARTISAN BAKERY

Arguably the finest bakery in San Francisco

1

2

FACING PAGE | **ELIXIR DESIGN** | ART DIRECTOR **JENNIFER JERDE** | DESIGNER **AARON CRUSE** | CLIENT **TARTINE**
1   **GRETEMAN GROUP** | DESIGNER **JAMES STRANGE** | CLIENT **WICHITA AVIATION FESTIVAL**
2   **GINGERBEE CREATIVE** | DESIGNER **GINGER KNAFF** | CLIENT **WEST MONT**

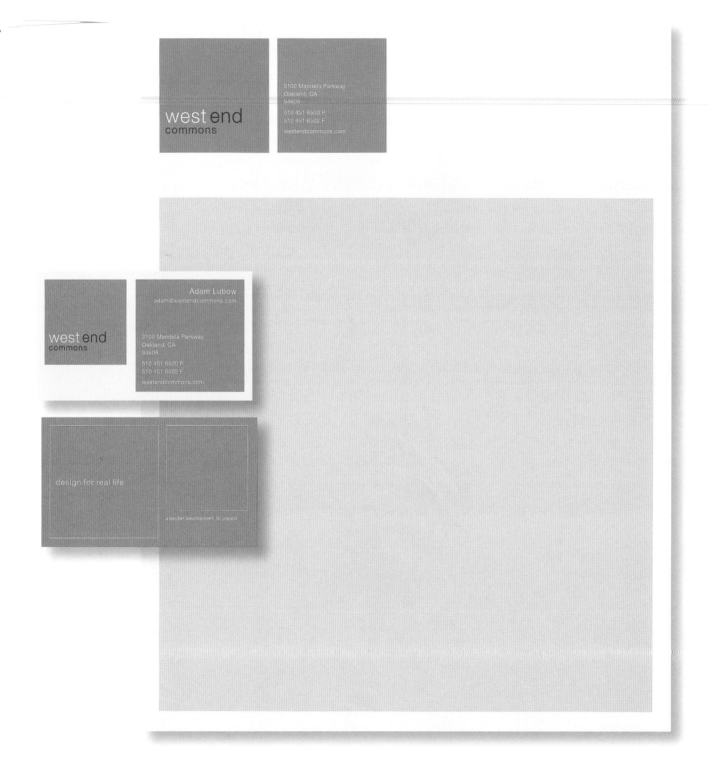

PUBLIC | ART DIRECTOR **TODD FOREMAN** | DESIGNERS **TODD FOREMAN, LINDSAY WHEELER** | CLIENT **POCKET DEVELOPMENT**

Tim
Foster
Architects

1 Purley Place, London, N1 1QA
Telephone 020 7354 1315
Fax 020 7226 8005

Email mail@timfosterarchitects.com
Web www.timfosterarchitects.com

Partners
Tim Foster
MA DipArch (Cantab) RIBA
Edmund Wilson
MA DipArch (Cantab) RIBA

Tim Foster Architects LLP is
a Limited Liability Partnership
Registered in England & Wales
Number OC305622
Registered Office
1 Purley Place, London, N1 1QA
VAT Number 242 7697 38

FORM | ART DIRECTOR PAULA BENSON | DESIGNERS PAULA BENSON, NICK HARD | CLIENT TIM FOSTER ARCHITECTS

1

2

APPAREL

1   TIM SMITH DESIGN | DESIGNER TIM SMITH | CLIENT TIM SMITH DESIGN
2   LLOYDS GRAPHIC DESIGN, LTD | DESIGNER ALEXANDER LLOYD | CLIENT PETE BAKER

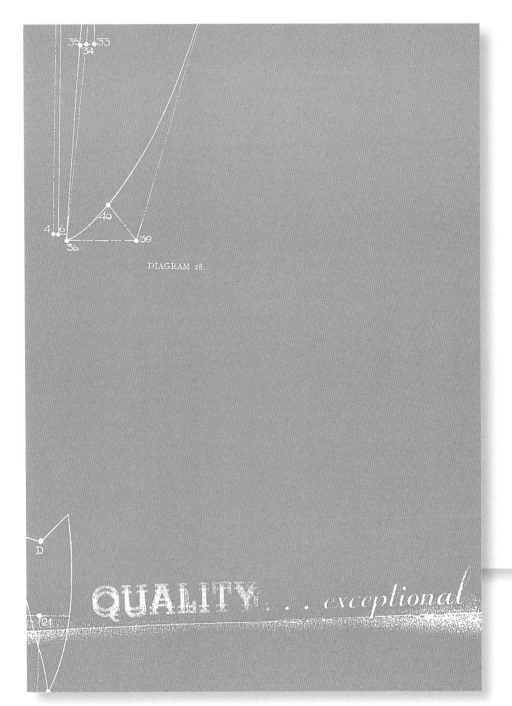

DIAGRAM 28.

QUALITY... *exceptional*

Tailors of Distinction

Hyde Park
246 Unley Road, Hyde Park
South Australia 5061
Telephone 08 8373 5658
Facsimile 08 8172 2176

David Jones
2nd Floor David Jones
100 Rundle Mall Adelaide 5000
Telephone 08 8305 3481

info@tailorsofdistinction.com
www.tailorsofdistinction.com

VOICE | DESIGNER **ANTHONY DELEO** | CLIENT **TAILORS OF DISTINCTION**
NEXT SPREAD | **KINETIC SINGAPORE** | ART DIRECTORS **ROY POH, PANN LIM** | DESIGNER **JONATHAN YUEN** | CLIENT **MIRACLE CREATIONS**

1

2

3

4

1   PIERRE RADEMAKER DESIGN | ART DIRECTOR PIERRE RADEMAKER | DESIGNERS PIERRE RADEMAKER, DEBBIE SHIBATA | CLIENT COAST NATIONAL BANK
2   BOY + GIRL DESIGN | DESIGNER TODD VERLANDER | CLIENT FOX BARREL HARD CIDER
3   PIERRE RADEMAKER DESIGN | ART DIRECTOR PIERRE RADEMAKER | DESIGNERS PIERRE RADEMAKER, KENNY SWETE | CLIENT CALIFORNIA POLYTECHNIC
     STATE UNIVERSITY
4   DOTZERO DESIGN | DESIGNERS JON WIPPICH, KAREN WIPPICH | CLIENT CITY OF PORTLAND WATER BUREAU

     FACING PAGE | GLITSCHKA STUDIOS | DESIGNER VON R. GLITSCHKA | CLIENT NW TATTOOS

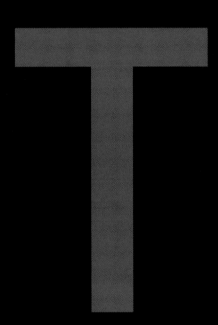

Typography: Type that moves you. Single letterforms, hand lettered logotypes, essay-laden letterheads, and elegant ligatures—these sixty works express a designer's love of letters. Though they share a common alphabet, each is unique in both form and meaning.

AUSTIN STUDIOS

TEXAS FILM HALL of FAME

AUSTIN FILM SOCIETY

OFFICE

512 322.0145 VOX
322.5192 FAX

1901 EAST **51** STREET | AUSTIN, TX **78723**

AFS @AUSTINFILM.ORG

AUSTIN FILM SOCIETY

STUDIO COORDINATOR
RACHEL BLACKNEY

AUSTIN STUDIOS

TEXAS FILM HALL of FAME

512 322.0145 VOX
322.5192 FAX

1901 EAST 51 STREET   AUSTIN, TEXAS 78723
RACHEL@AUSTINFILM.ORG

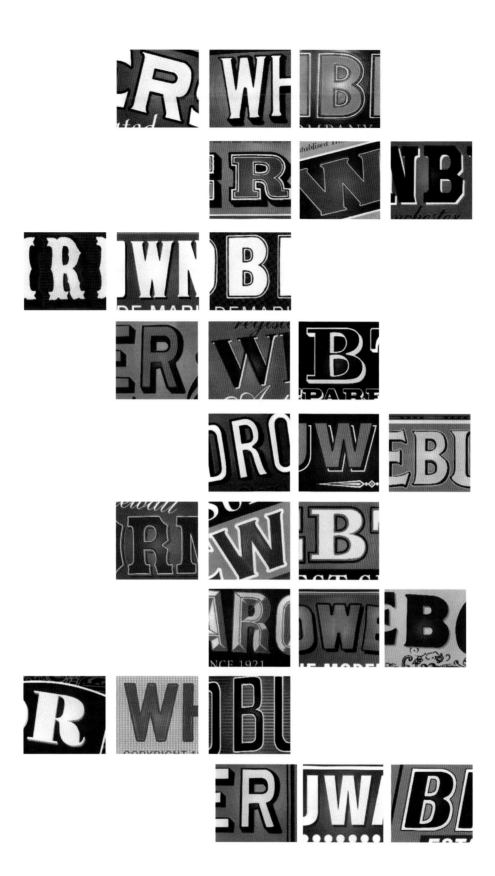

FACING PAGE | **MARC ENGLISH DESIGN** | DESIGNER **MARC ENGLISH** | CLIENT **AUSTIN FILM SOCIETY**
LOWERCASE, INC. | ART DIRECTOR **TIM BRUCE** | DESIGNERS **TIM BRUCE, KRIS MCKNIGHT** | CLIENT **RIVER WEST BRANDS, LLC**

standard

1

INVIA

2

GWARSH

3

ME,ME

FACING PAGE | GARDNER DESIGN | DESIGNER **LUKE BOTT** | CLIENT **STANDARD**
1 CESART | ART DIRECTOR **JEAN-FRANÇOIS CLERMONT** | CLIENT **CESART / INVIA**
2 ART DIRECTOR **JOEL WASSERMAN** | CLIENT **GWARSH**
3 ME,ME | DESIGNER **PETER VATTANATHAM** | CLIENT **ME,ME**

Level 46, MLC Centre
19-29 Martin Place
Sydney NSW 2000
ACN 099 055 571

Telephone: 61 2 9367 0888
Facsimile: 61 2 9367 0896
Email: base@basebackpackers.com
Web: www.basebackpackers.com

base
BACKPACKERS

base
BACKPACKERS

Graeme Warring CEO
Mobile: 0411 250 425

EVERY TRAVELLER NEEDS A BASE

1

2

3

FACING PAGE | BILLY BLUE CREATIVE | DESIGNER JUSTIN SMITH | CLIENT BASE BACKPACKERS
1   IAAH /IAMALWAYSHUNGRY | DESIGNER NESSIM HIGSON | CLIENT DC COMICS
2   STUDIO SONSOLES LLORENS | DESIGNER STUDIO SONSOLES LLORENS | CLIENT LA CLARA
3   DAMION HICKMAN DESIGN | ART DIRECTOR DAMION HICKMAN | DESIGNERS DAMION HICKMAN, LEIGHTON HUBBELL | CLIENT TEN RESTAURANT GROUP

1

2

3

4

1   UP DESIGN BUREAU | DESIGNER CHRIS PARKS | CLIENT BARRY SANDERS
2   DESIGN AHEAD | DESIGNER RALF STUMPF | CLIENT STEINBRUCH
3   FORM | DESIGNERS PAUL WEST, PAULA BENSON | CLIENT FORM
4   HULA + HULA | ART DIRECTORS OUIOUE OLLERVIDES & CHA! | DESIGNER OUIOUE OLLERVIDES | CLIENT KONG
    FACING PAGE | SAGMEISTER, INC. | ART DIRECTOR STEFAN SAGMEISTER | DESIGNER MATTHIAS ERNSTBERGER | CLIENT LOU REED

LOU REED

584 BROADWAY suite 609

NEW YORK, NY 10012

212 343 2100

212 343 2127 fax

SISTER RAY ENTERPRISES

sisraynyc@sisterray.com

www.loureed.com

DEPARTURE DATE

ORIGIN

PASSENGER NAME

DESTINATION

6151 Portage Rd.   Portage MI 49002   USA   North America   42° 13-25' N x 85° 33-50' W   Earth   Milky Way

COORDINATES
6151 Portage Rd.   Portage MI 49002   USA   North America   Earth   Milky Way
866 5-AIRZOO
269 382-6555 p
269 382-1813 f
www.airzoo.org

1

me&b.
MATERNITY

2

3

SCEATS

4

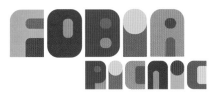

5

FOBIA
picnic

FACING PAGE | JAGER GROUP | ART DIRECTOR ROB JACKSON | DESIGNER ELENA TISLERIES | CLIENT AIR ZOO AVIATION MUSEUM
1   LISKA + ASSOCIATES | ART DIRECTOR TANYA QUICK | DESIGNER DANIELLE AKSTEIN | CLIENT ME&B MATERNITY
2   HULA + HULA | ART DIRECTORS OUIOUE OLLERVIDES & CHA! | DESIGNER OUIOUE OLLERVIDES | CLIENT BMG ENTERTAINMENT
3   DESIGNER JOEL WASSERMAN | CLIENT SCEATS KNECT
4   BE.DESIGN | ART DIRECTOR WILL BURKE | DESIGNER MONICA SCHLAUG | CLIENT PEKOE SIPHOUSE
5   HULA + HULA | ART DIRECTORS OUIOUE OLLERVIDES & CHA! | DESIGNER OUIOUE OLLERVIDES | CLIENT FOBIA

deb markanton   certified massage therapist   415 835 4759
2906 lyon street   san francisco   california   94123

levitate

levitate

deb markanton   certified massage therapist   415 835 4759
2906 lyon street   san francisco   california   94123

a note for you

levitate

CIRCLE K STUDIO | DESIGNER JULIE KEENAN | CLIENT LEVITATE
FACING PAGE | ST. IVES / CREATIVE SIDE | DESIGNER JEFF KINCAID | CLIENT ST. IVES

St Ives

creative side

A DESIGN STUDIO | Photography | Graphic Design | Copy

MIAMI
13449 NW 42nd Avenue Miami, FL 33054
(305) 685-7381
stivescreative.com

NEW YORK
75 Ninth Ave 2nd floor New York, NY 10011
(212) 414-7506
stivescreative.com

St Ives Creative Side
13449 NW 42nd Avenue Miami, FL 33054
(305) 685-7381
stivescreative.com

1

2

3

4

1   KINETIC SINGAPORE | ART DIRECTORS PANN LIM, ROY POH | DESIGNER PANN LIM | CLIENT AMARA HOLDINGS LIMITED
2   NOON | ART DIRECTOR CINTHIA WEN | DESIGNER CLAUDIA FUNG | CLIENT CARBON NYC
3   LISKA + ASSOCIATES | ART DIRECTOR TANYA QUICK | DESIGNER JONATHAN SEEDS | CLIENT LUXI
4   KENDALL ROSS | ART DIRECTOR DAVID KENDALL | DESIGNER SCOTT FRIESEN | CLIENT SUKRA YOGA
     FACING PAGE | FORM | ART DIRECTOR PAUL WEST | DESIGNERS PAUL WEST, CHRIS HILTON | CLIENT DARKSIDE FX

DarksideFX

Shepperton Studios Studios Road Shepperton Middlesex TW17 0QD
Telephone: +44 (0)7000 327574 Fax: +44 (0)7002 327574
Email: info@darksidefx.com www.darksidefx.com
Directors: Joss Williams Mike Dawson Registered Office: Beachey House 87 Church Street
Crowthorne Berks RG45 7AW Registered in England No: 345662 VAT: 669447974

PUBLIC ARCHITECTURE

PUTS THE RESOURCES OF ARCHITECTURE IN THE SERVICE OF THE
PUBLIC INTEREST. WE IDENTIFY AND SOLVE PRACTICAL PROBLEMS
OF HUMAN INTERACTION IN THE BUILT ENVIRONMENT AND ACT AS
A CATALYST FOR PUBLIC DISCOURSE THROUGH EDUCATION,
ADVOCACY AND THE DESIGN OF PUBLIC SPACES AND AMENITIES.
1126 FOLSOM STREET, No. 3, SAN FRANCISCO, CA 94103-1397
T 415.861.8200 F 415.431.9695 WWW.PUBLICARCHITECTURE.ORG

PUBLIC ARCHITECTURE
PUTS THE RESOURCES OF ARCHITECTURE IN THE SERVICE OF THE
PUBLIC INTEREST. WE IDENTIFY AND SOLVE PRACTICAL PROBLEMS
OF HUMAN INTERACTION IN THE BUILT ENVIRONMENT AND ACT AS
A CATALYST FOR PUBLIC DISCOURSE THROUGH EDUCATION,
ADVOCACY AND THE DESIGN OF PUBLIC SPACES AND AMENITIES.
1126 FOLSOM STREET, No. 3, SAN FRANCISCO, CA 94103-1397
T 415.861.8200 F 415.431.9695 WWW.PUBLICARCHITECTURE.ORG

John Peterson, AIA
Chairman

jpeterson@publicarchitecture.org

1

association
internationale des
critiques d'art, turquie
international association
of art critics, turkey
uluslararası sanat
eleştirmenleri derneği,
türkiye

AICA
TR

2

PUNCHCUT

3

R O U T L E D G E
M O D I S E
M O S S   ATTORNEYS
M O R R I S

FACING PAGE | MENDE DESIGN | DESIGNER JEREMY MENDE | CLIENT PUBLIC ARCHITECTURE
1 DESIGNER | UMUT SÜDÜAK | CLIENT INTERNATIONAL ASSOCIATION OF ART CRITICS, TURKEY
2 PUNCHCUT | ART DIRECTOR JARED BENSON | DESIGNERS J. BENSON, J. PEMBERTON, K. OLEWILER | CLIENT PUNCHCUT
3 ENTERPRISE IG | ART DIRECTOR DAVE HOLLAND | DESIGNERS ADAM BOTHA, DAVE HOLLAND | CLIENT ROUTLEDGE MODISE MOSS MORRIS

MGMT. DESIGN | ART DIRECTORS **ARIEL APTE, SARAH GEPHART, ALICIA CHENG** | DESIGNERS **ARIEL APTE, SARAH GEPHART** | CLIENT **MGMT.DESIGN**

1

2

3

4

view

1   BÜROCRATIK | DESIGNER **ADRIANO ESTEVES** | CLIENT **CAPA, SOCIEDADE DE ADVOGADOS, LDA.**
2   **SALT BRANDING** | ART DIRECTOR **PAUL PARKIN** | DESIGNER **CESAR CHIN** | CLIENT **ALIPH**
3   **OFFICE FOR DESIGN** | DESIGNER **PAULA ALBANY** | CLIENT **INDONA**
4   **WEMAKE DESIGN** | DESIGNER **NIK DILLON** | CLIENT **VIEW MAGAZINE**

POLSHEK PARTNERSHIP **ARCHITECTS**

Joseph L. Fleischer FAIA Timothy P. Hartung FAIA Duncan R. Hazard AIA Richard M. Olcott FAIA James S. Polshek FAIA Susan T. Rodriguez AIA Todd H. Schliemann AIA

Duncan R. Hazard AIA
Partner

Polshek Partnership LLP
320 West 13th Street
New York, New York 10014.1278
212.807.7171 tel
212.807.5917 fax
www.polshek.com

11628 santa monica blvd #9 west los angeles ca 90025 **T 310.207.5160** F 310.207.5220  www.nookbistro.com

FACING PAGE | **POULIN + MORRIS, INC.** | DESIGNER **L. RICHARD POULIN** | CLIENT **POLSHEK PARTNERSHIP**
THIS PAGE | **PH.D** | ART DIRECTORS **CLIVE PIERCY, MICHAEL HODGSON** | DESIGNERS **CAROL KONO-NOBLE, CLIVE PIERCY** | CLIENT **NOOK BISTRO**
NEXT SPREAD, LEFT | **POULIN + MORRIS, INC.** | DESIGNERS **DOUGLAS MORRIS, L. RICHARD POULIN** | CLIENT **TUCCI, SEGRETE & ROSEN**
NEXT SPREAD, RIGHT | **VOICE** | DESIGNERS **ANTHONY DELEO, SCOTT CARSLAKE** | CLIENT **DAYCORP PROPERTY DEVELOPERS**

TUCCI | SEGRETE + ROSEN

Dominick L. Segrete, AIA

Edward M. Calabrese
Lisa Contreras
Evangelo Dascal
Mike L. Kirn
Anthony Macahilig
Brett A. Rosenfeld
Santo Zappala

Architecture. Planning. Design

Tucci Segrete and Rosen Consultants, Inc. 475 Tenth Avenue New York, New York 10018 t.212.629.3900 f.212.629.3907 info@TSRNY.com

555 The Parade Magill SA 5072 **TELEPHONE** 08-8331-2533 **FACSIMILE** 08-8331-2544 **EMAIL** travisd@senet.com.au **ACN** 008-123-742

DAYCORP PROPERTY DEVELOPMENT

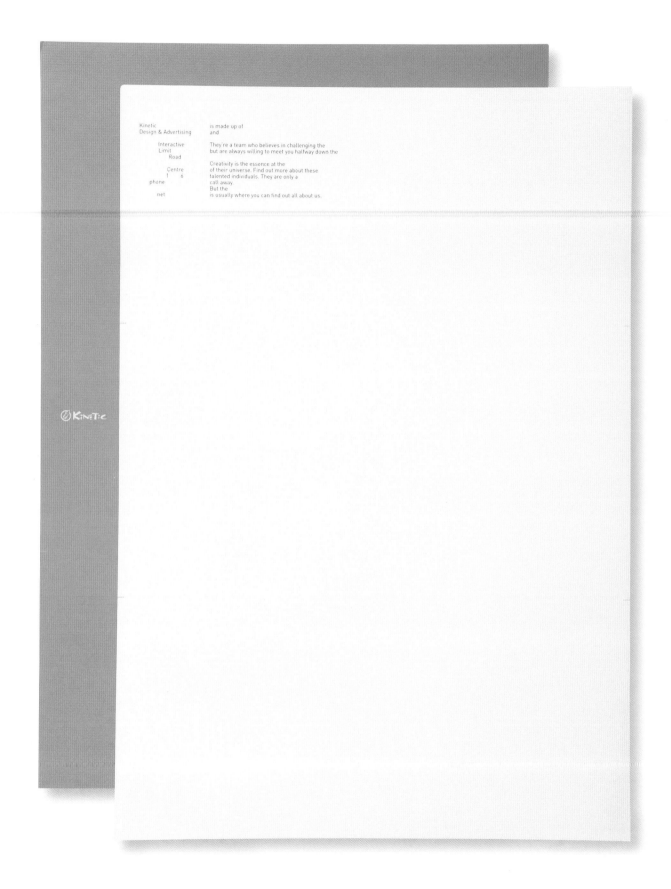

Kinetic
Design & Advertising

Interactive
Limit
Road

Centre
1   6
phone

net

is made up of
and

They're a team who believes in challenging the
but are always willing to meet you halfway down the

Creativity is the essence at the
of their universe. Find out more about these
talented individuals. They are only a
call away.
But the
is usually where you can find out all about us.

KINETIC SINGAPORE | ART DIRECTORS **PANN LIM, ROY POH, LENG SOH** | DESIGNER **LENG SOH** | CLIENT **KINETIC SINGAPORE**
FACING PAGE | **FIREFLY STUDIO PTE LTD** | ART DIRECTOR **MOHD YAZID** | DESIGNERS **LENG SOH BRICE LI, NORMAN LI** | CLIENT **FIREFLY STUDIO PTE LTD**

Firefly

firefly | *retail*

Terry Lee
MANAGING DIRECTOR
MBA

ADDRESS
161 Neil Road Level Two
Singapore 088885

PHONE
6324 6369

FACSIMILE
6324 3477

MOBILE
9451 3041

EMAIL
terry@firefly.com.sg

WEBSITE
www.firefly.com.sg

CREATIVITY SPARKS INGENUITY

Member of First Media Group of Companies
Reg. No. 200106320H

FIREFLY STUDIO PTE LTD

ADDRESS
161 Neil Road
Level Two
Singapore 088885

PHONE
6324 6369

FACSIMILE
6324 3477

EMAIL
contact@firefly.com.sg

WEBSITE
www.firefly.com.sg

PUBLIC | ART DIRECTOR **TODD FOREMAN** | DESIGNER **NANCY THOMAS** | CLIENT **DAVID STARK WILSON**

THE dub HOUSE
qnp

DIGITAL MEDIA DUPLICATION

MAILING ADDRESS (915 Northeast 20 Avenue Suite 4
Fort Lauderdale, Florida 33304

Telephone 954.524.3658
CONTACT (Toll Free 877.900.DUBS (3827)
Facsimile 954.522.1905

INTERNET (info@thedubhouse.net
www.thedubhouse.net

THE dub HOUSE   Suzanne Sousa
qnp   DIRECTOR OF
                    SALES DEVELOPMENT

MAILING ADDRESS (915 Northeast 20 Avenue Suite 4
Fort Lauderdale, Florida 33304

Telephone 954.524.3658
CONTACT (Toll Free 877.900.DUBS (3827)
Facsimile 954.522.1905

INTERNET (suzanne@thedubhouse.net
www.thedubhouse.net

1

modoi

2

bamboo ®

3

pointlet

FACING PAGE | GOUTHIER DESIGN | CLIENT THE DUB HOUSE
1   GENE LEE DESIGN | DESIGNER GENE LEE | CLIENT MODOI
2   LANDOR ASSOCIATES | ART DIRECTOR NICOLAS APARICIO | DESIGNERS ANDREW OTTO, PHIL FOSTER | CLIENT MUNCHKIN
3   GRAPEFRUIT | ART DIRECTOR MARIUS URSACHE | DESIGNER ANDREI BOTEZ | CLIENT POINTLET

1

2

3

4

1   UP DESIGN BUREAU | ART DIRECTOR CHRIS PARKS | DESIGNERS CHRIS PARKS, CHANEY KIMBELL | CLIENT UP DESIGN BUREAU
2   GEYRHALTER DESIGN | ART DIRECTOR FABIAN GEYRHALTER | DESIGNER EVELYN KIM | CLIENT ZANGPO
3   OAKLEY DESIGN STUDIOS | DESIGNER TIM OAKLEY | CLIENT KINK FM 102 - PORTLAND
4   IAAH /IAMALWAYSHUNGRY | DESIGNER NESSIM HIGSON | CLIENT ROBERTSON AND WILLIAMS FURNITURE DESIGN

9R

Ninah Consulting

With compliments

9R

Ninah Consulting

Bridge House
63-65 North Wharf Road
London W2 1LA

t +44 (0) 20 7224 8510
f +44 (0) 20 7298 6920

e info@ninah.com
www.ninah.com

Bridge House
63-65 North Wharf Road
London W2 1LA

t +44 (0) 20 7224 8510
f +44 (0) 20 7298 6920

e info@ninah.com
www.ninah.com

Registered in England No. 1921320
Registered office as above
VAT No. GB 707 2836 33

DIALOG | ART DIRECTOR **DAVID LOCK** | DESIGNERS **DAVID LOCK, JOE P MORGAN** | CLIENT **NINAH CONSULTING**

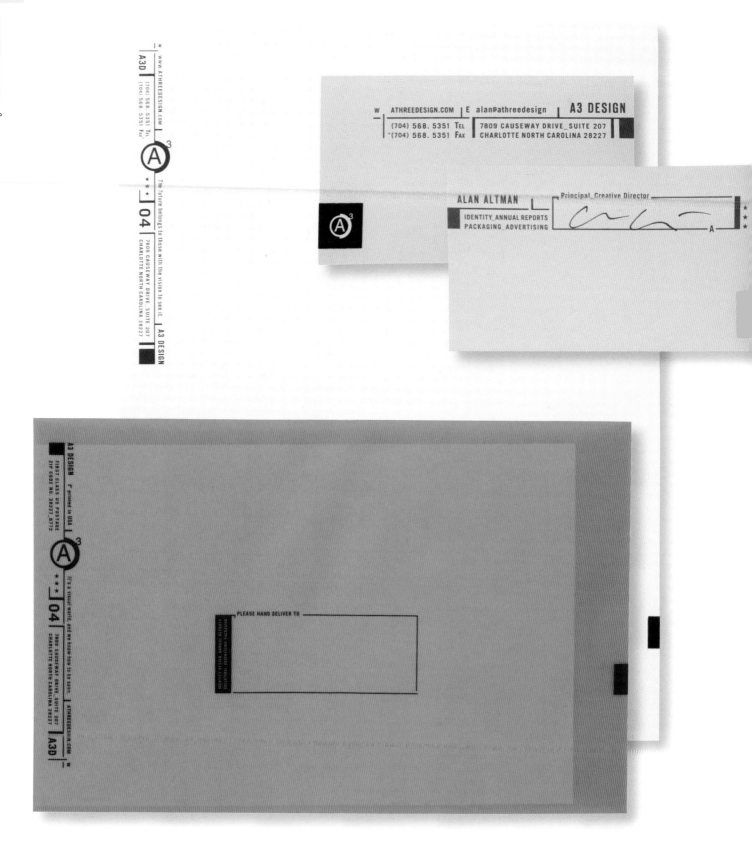

1

2

INTERACTION ·ONLY

3

1   **FORM** | ART DIRECTOR **PAUL WEST** | DESIGNERS **NICK HARD, PAUL WEST** | CLIENT **DAZED / TOPSHOP**
2   **CAVE DESIGN** | DESIGNER **LEO DIAZ** | CLIENT **INTERACTION ONLY CONFERENCE**
3   **MDG** | ART DIRECTOR **TIM MERRY** | DESIGNER **MIKE EATON** | CLIENT **MDG**

Materiality: The medium really is the message. In these examples, paper, texture, die cuts, and folds play an integral role in the success of the design. Each is an experience made more acute through the creative art of production.

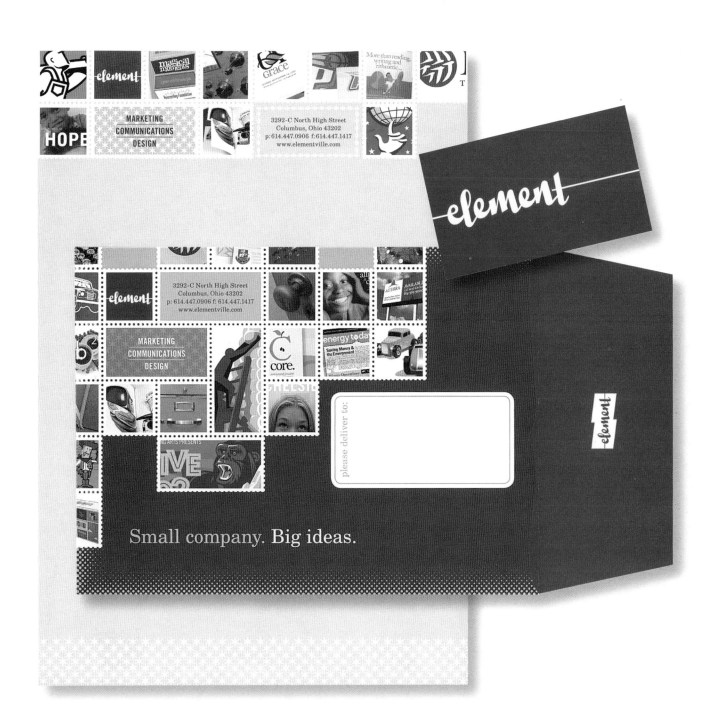

ELEMENT | ART DIRECTOR **JEREMY SLAGLE** | DESIGNERS **JEREMY SLAGLE, JOHN MCCOLLUM** | CLIENT **ELEMENT**

PING-PONG DESIGN | ART DIRECTORS BARRY DE BRUIJN, MAARTEN JURRIAANSE | DESIGNERS BARRY DE BRUIJN, MAARTEN JURRIAANSE
| CLIENT MAURITS DE BRUIJN

PH.D | ART DIRECTORS CLIVE PIERCY, MICHAEL HODGSON | DESIGNERS CLIVE PIERCY, JOHN HUGHES | CLIENT FATHER'S OFFICE

UniForm®
47 Tabernacle Street
London EC2A 4AA, UK
Telephone: +44 (0)20 7014 1433
Fax: +44 (0)20 7014 1431
Email: studio@uniform.uk.com
Web: uniform.uk.com

Partners: P Benson, P West. VAT No: 523 4071 79
UniForm® is a registered trademark

UniForm®
47 Tabernacle Street
London EC2A 4AA, UK
Telephone: +44 (0)20 7014 1433
Fax: +44 (0)20 7014 1431
Email: studio@uniform.uk.com
Web: uniform.uk.com

Partners: P Benson, P West. VAT No: 523 4071 79
UniForm® is a registered trademark

FACING PAGE | **FORM** | ART DIRECTORS **PAULA BENSON, PAUL WEST** | DESIGNERS **PAULA BENSON, NICK HARD, PAUL WEST** | CLIENT **UNIFORM**
HEATH KANE DESIGN | DESIGNER **HEATH KANE** | CLIENT **ZEBRA PEOPLE**

Campaign for PICA	Letterhead

Portland Institute for Contemporary Art
Address: 720 SW Washington, Suite 700, Portland, OR 97205
Phone: 503.242.1419   Fax: 503.243.1167   Email: pica@pica.org
Web: www.pica.org

Campaign for PICA	Card

Portland Institute for Contemporary Art
Address: 720 SW Washington, Suite 700, Portland, OR 97205
Phone: 503.242.1419   Fax: 503.243.1167
Email: pica@pica.org   Web: www.pica.org

What is art?

THE CAMPAIGN FOR PICA
CAMPAIGN LEADERSHIP

Dan Wieden, Wieden & Kennedy
Honorary Co-Chair

Bob Gerding, Gerding Development
Honorary Co-Chair

Kristy Edmunds
Executive Director and Curator

Megan Brooke
Victoria Frey
Peter Gray
Pat Harrington
Kathleen Lewis
Mike Lindberg
Alice McCartor
Martha Richards
Joan Shipley
Verne Stanford
Linda Taylor

PICA BOARD OF TRUSTEES
Joan Shipley (Chair)
Pat Harrington (Vice Chair)
Dennis Johnson (Treasurer)
Alice McCartor (Secretary)
Gene d'Autremont
Francesca Frost DesCamp
Leslie B. Durst
Bart Eberwein
Kristy Edmunds
Victoria Frey
John Jay
Kathleen Lewis
Julie Mancini
Rod Pulliam
Chris Riley
Miriam Rose
Howard Shapiro
Kathleen Stephenson-Kuhn
Francien Valk
Dorie Vollum
Ann Wellman
Kaie Wellman
Jim Winkler
Steve Wynne
Paul Zumwalt

NATIONAL ADVISORY BOARD
Edward Albee
Chris Bruce
Gordon Gilkey
Philip Glass
Linda Greenberg
Carol Hepper
Robert Lyons
Mark Murphy
Peter Sellars
Melissa Schiff Soros
Robert Soros
Rebecca Stewart
Sally Stillman
Elizabeth Streb
John S. Weber
Dan Wieden

1

2

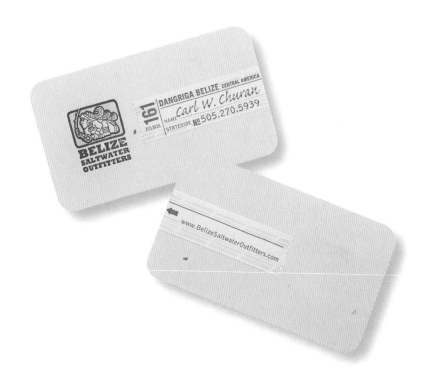

1   MICHAEL POWELL DESIGN | DESIGNER MICHAEL POWELL | CLIENT MICHAEL POWELL DESIGN
2   RICK JOHNSON & COMPANY | ART DIRECTOR SAM MACLAY | DESIGNER TIM MCGRATH | CLIENT BELIZE SALTWATER OUTFITTERS

GRETEMAN GROUP | ART DIRECTORS SONIA GRETEMAN, JAMES STRANGE | DESIGNERS JAMES STRANGE, CRAIG TOMSON | CLIENT KANSAS STATE FAIR

1

2

1   JAGER GROUP | DESIGNER ROB JACKSON | CLIENT OUTDOOR ADVERTISING ASSOC. OF AMERICA
2   ISOTOPE 221 | DESIGNER CHRISTOPHER CANNON | CLIENT BRIDGE NINE RECORDS

SUBPLOT DESIGN INC.
The Mercantile Building, 318 Homer Street, Suite 301
Vancouver, British Columbia, Canada V6B 2V2
Telephone 604 685 2990 Facsimile 604 685 2909
www.subplot.com

SUBPLOT DESIGN INC. | ART DIRECTOR **MATTHEW CLARK** | DESIGNERS **ROY WHITE, MATTHEW CLARK** | CLIENT **SUBPLOT DESIGN**

ALAN OWINGS XT.24

415.695.0110 T
415.695.0379 F
alan@lundbergdesign.com
2620 THIRD ST, SAN FRANCISCO, CA 94107-3115

LUNDBERGDESIGN

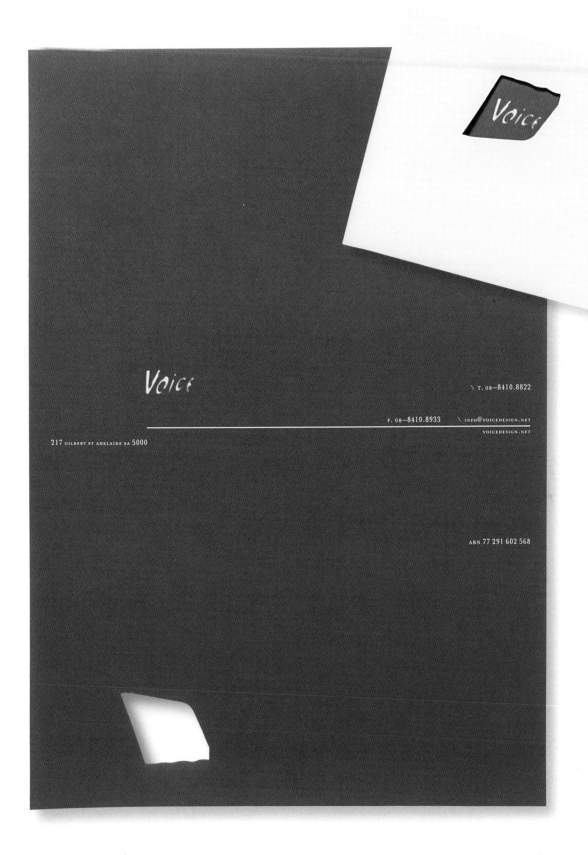

Voice

217 GILBERT ST ADELAIDE SA 5000

\ T. 08—8410.8822

F. 08—8410.8933   \ INFO@VOICEDESIGN.NET
VOICEDESIGN.NET

ABN 77 291 602 568

JOINT

Sam Selis
317 SW Alder, Suite 507
Portland, OR 97204
503.525.4630
Fax 503.525.4633

JOINT

Sibylle Jensen

TASCHENMANUFAKTUR

Sibylle Jensen · Püttmannsweg 11 · 44803 Bochum

Sibylle Jensen

TASCHENMANUFAKTUR

Püttmannsweg 11 · 44803 Bochum
T + F 02 34·4 38 50 46 · info@wunschtasche.de

Püttmannsweg 11 · 44803 Bochum · T + F 02 34·4 38 50 46 · info@wunschtasche.de
Sparkasse Bochum · Kto. 1 475 532 · BLZ 430 500 01

TRACY DESIGN | ART DIRECTOR **JAN TRACY** | DESIGNER **PATRICK SIMONE** | CLIENT **BLACK BOX ADVERTISING**

THE
MODERN BALL
'05

THE MODE...
SAN FRANCISCO
151 THIRD

SFMOMA

HELEN SCHWAB
Chairman

SAN FRANCISCO
MUSEUM OF MODERN ART
151 THIRD STREET
SAN FRANCISCO, CA 94103
TEL 415-357-4021

ELIXIR DESIGN | ART DIRECTOR **JENNIFER JERDE** | DESINGER **NATHAN DURRANT** | CLIENT **SAN FRANCISCO MUSEUM OF MODERN ART**

1

2

1   LOGIENT | ART DIRECTOR PHILIPPE ARCHOUTAKIS | DESIGNER CARLOS PONCE | CLIENT LOGIENT
2   FIREFLY STUDIO PTE LTD | ART DIRECTOR MOHD YAZID | DESIGNER NORMAN LI | CLIENT FIRST MEDIA PTE LTD

FLORIDA'S FORECLOSURE ALTERNATIVE LLC
PROTECTING YOUR INVESTMENT IN YOUR HOME

JEFF KROOP
PRESIDENT

FLORIDA'S FORECLOSURE ALTERNATIVE LLC
PROTECTING YOUR INVESTMENT IN YOUR HOME

FREE GIFTS

*$500.00 FREE EMERGENCY CASH
** $40 WORTH OF COUPONS FOR GAS, DINING, OR MOVIES

THESE FREE GIFTS ARE FOR ALLOWING US TO PRESENT OUR FREE **NO OBLIGATION PROPOSAL.** AFTER WE MAKE OUR PROPOSAL, YOU CAN EITHER ACCEPT OUR HELP OR REJECT IT. **IT IS YOUR CHOICE,** BUT THE GIFTS WILL BE YOURS TO KEEP.

WE CAN PROVIDE THE FUNDING TO END YOUR FORECLOSURE.

CALL NOW! TIME IS OF THE ESSENCE! **(954) 720-4371**

* 10, $50 coupons redeemed monthly
** 4, $10 coupons redeemed quarterly

The Design Center
at Philadelphia University

the design center

The Goldie Paley House   4200 Henry Avenue   Philadelphia, Pennsylvania 19144-5497
tel 215.951.2860   *fax* 215.951.2662   thedesigncenter@philau.edu

The Design Center
at Philadelphia University

George H. Marcus   *Guest Curator*

4200 Henry Avenue
Philadelphia, Pennsylvania 19144-5497
tel 215.732.4297   *fax* 215.951.2662
gmarcus@ix.netcom.com

the design center

The Design Center
at Philadelphia University

the design center

The Goldie Paley House
4200 Henry Avenue
Philadelphia, Pennsylvania 19144-5497

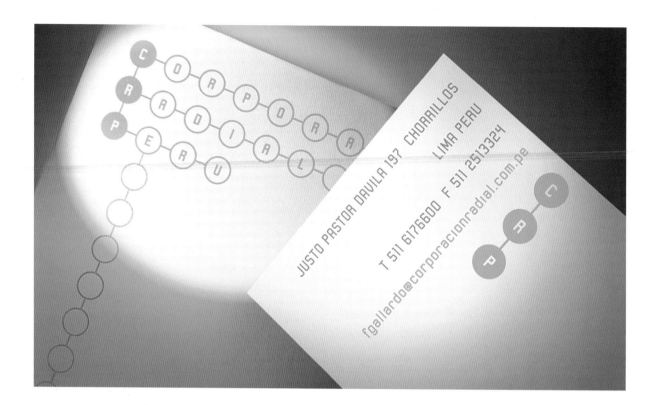

STUDIO A | ART DIRECTORS **ENA ANDRADE, MARÍA JOSÉ BUSTAMANTE** | DESIGNER **CLAUDIA JENSSEN** | CLIENT **CORPORACIÓN RADIAL DEL PERÚ - CRP**
FACING PAGE | Ó! | DESIGNER **EINAR GYLFASON** | CLIENT Ó!

Ó!
Grafisk hönnun
Holtsgötu 19
101 Reykjavík

EINAR GYLFASON
Hönnuður/FÍT
840 0220
einar@oid.is
www.oid.is

Ó!
Grafisk hönnun
Holtsgötu 19
101 Reykjavík

840 0220
oid@oid.is
www.oid.is

Miscellany: Odds and ends. As with any effort to categorize a unique collection of creative work, there are those examples that simply do not fit within the conventions we have established. The following is a selection of the eclectic, the meritorious, and the otherwise indefinably interesting.

1

SUTRA
LOUNGE

2

3

LES ALIMENTS FINS
LE DUC

4

FACING PAGE | MAKE SALISBURY LLC | ART DIRECTOR MIKE SALISBURY | DESIGNERS TOR NORHEIM, DERIK HARVIN | CLIENT HALO
1   DAMION HICKMAN DESIGN | DESIGNER DAMION HICKMAN | CLIENT SUTRA LOUNGE
2   TRUMPET | ART DIRECTOR PAT MCGUINESS | CLIENT REAL MEX
3   IRIDIUM | DESIGNER JEAN-LUC DENAT | CLIENT LES ALIMENTS FINS LE DUC
4   LANDOR ASSOCIATES | ART DIRECTOR RACHEL WEAR | DESINGERS GRAHAM ATKINSON, ANDY KEENE | CLIENT FED EX SERVICE

1

THE FRENCH REVOLUTION

2

MILITARY HISTORY CHANNEL™

3

1   RED HERRING DESIGN | DESIGNER NATHAN SAVAGE | CLIENT THE HISTORY CHANNEL
2   RED HERRING DESIGN | DESIGNER NATHAN SAVAGE | CLIENT THE HISTORY CHANNEL
3   WOW! BRANDING | ART DIRECTOR PERRY CHUA | CLIENT BEAVER AIRCRAFT
     FACING PAGE | DESIGN AHEAD | DESIGNER AXEL VOSS | CLIENT AUTOMOTIV

Michael Kühe
Geschäftsführer

www.auto-motiv.com

Unterdorfstr. 27 | D-45143 Essen
Tel +49(201) 82 33 80 | Fax +49(201) 82 13 22

Mobile (0172) 2 13 03 05
kueke@auto-motiv.com

AutoMotiv - Gemeinschaft zur Durchführung dynamischer Prozesse

1

2

3

1   PINXIT | ART DIRECTOR EROS RIGOLI | DESIGNER RICCARDO CRESTA | CLIENT LE ANTICHE MURA SRL
2   PIERRE RADEMAKER DESIGN | ART DIRECTOR PIERRE RADEMAKER | DESIGNERS PIERRE RADEMAKER, DEBBIE SHIBATA | CLIENT WINTER CONSTRUCTION
3   PIERRE RADEMAKER DESIGN | ART DIRECTOR PIERRE RADEMAKER | DESIGNERS PIERRE RADEMAKER, DEBBIE SHIBATA | CLIENT CITY OF SOLVANG

1

THE CAMPUS
at Rancho Oaks

2

PINE
WOODS

3

1   DAMION HICKMAN DESIGN | DESIGNER DAMION HICKMAN | CLIENT MASTER DEVELOPMENT CORP.
2   SKY DESIGN | ART DIRECTOR W. TODD VAUGHT | DESINGER CARRIE WALLACE BROWN | CLIENT PINEWOODS
3   FUEL INC. | ART DIRECTOR BOB ZEIDLER | DESINGERS BILL BOLLMAN, LANCE LETHCOE | CLIENT JOHN DEERE CONSTRUCTION & FORESTRY

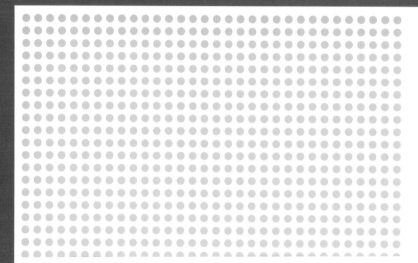

Form®

47 Tabernacle Street
London EC2A 4AA, UK

Telephone: +44 (0)20 7014 1430
Fax: +44 (0)20 7014 1431
ISDN: +44 (0)20 7014 1432

Email: studio@form.uk.com
Web: www.form.uk.com

114 rue ambroise croizat 93200 st denis france
ᴛ +33 (0) 1 55 84 02 50 ꜰ +33 (0) 1 55 84 02 63
w espace114.com

ESPACE 114

une opération immobilière de MSP PARIS SAS

FACING PAGE | **FORM** | ART DIRECTORS **PAUL WEST, PAULA BENSON** | DESINGERS **NICK HARD, PAUL WEST, PAULA BENSON** | CLIENT **FORM**
CONCRETE | ART DIRECTOR **JILLY SIMONS** | DESIGNERS **JILLY SIMONS, MARGARET MIEDLAR** | CLIENT **LUMIERE**

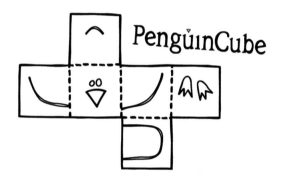

1

2

1 MONDERER DESIGN | ART DIRECTOR STEWART MONDERER | DESIGNER JASON CK MILLER | CLIENT DEAN COLLEGE
2 VERLANDER DESIGN | DESINGER MARK VERLANDER | CLIENT LUDICROUS HARDCORE ENERGY

DIRECTORY

82 **YUMI MATSUZAKI**
140 St. James Place, Apt #3F
Brooklyn, NY 11238 USA
917.628.3978
718.623.9117
aur3tx@hotmail.com

26, 193 **MDG**
13 Water Street
Holliston, MA 01746 USA
508.429.0755
508.429.0766
meaton@m-d-g.com

163 **ME. ME**
4420 Overland Ave. Suite A
Culver City, CA 90230 USA
310.558.9659
v@hellomeme.com

37 **MEATON DOT NET**
67 Upland Road
Attleboro, MA 02703 USA
617.460.4960
meaton@meaton.net

128, 138, **MENDE DESIGN**
140, 174, 1126 Folsom, #3
210 San Francisco, CA 94103 USA
415.309.8165
415.431.9695
jeremy@mendedesign.com

32, 39, **MERYL POLLEN DESIGN**
117 6059 Metropolitan Plaza
Los Angeles, CA 90036 USA
323.571.3898
323.571.3897
mpollen@comcast.net

58, 60, **METHOD ART & DESIGN**
106 2427 W. 25th St. N.
Wichita, KS 67204 USA
316.210.3272
316.838.4435
methodartanddesign@cox.net

176 **MGMT. DESIGN**
55 Washington Street, #704
Brooklyn, NY 11201
718.855.6262
718.855.6579
alicia@mgmtdesign.com

203 **MICHAEL POWELL DESIGN**
88 Union Avenue, Suite 105
Memphis, TN 38103 USA
901.578.7898
901.578.7878
mike@michaelpowelldesign
.com

224 **MIKE SALISBURY LLC**
P. O. Box 2309
Venice, CA 90294 USA
310.392.8779
310.392.9488
mikesalcom@aol.com

88, 100 **MILCH DESIGN**
Baader Str. 19
Munich 80469 Germany
0049 89 520466-0
0049189 520466-21
judith-may@milch-design.de

9, 10, 11, **MINE™**
12, 13 190 Putnam St.
San Francisco, CA 94110 USA
415 647 6463
cchs@minesf.com

95, 234 **MONDERER DESIGN**
2067 Massachusetts Ave.
Cambridge, MA 02140 USA
617.661.6125
stewart@monderer.com

120, 133 **MORTENSEN DESIGN INC**
416 Bush Street
Mountain View, CA 94041 USA
650.988.0946
650.988.0926
gordon@mortdes.com

94 **NINA DAVID
KOMMUNIKATIONSDESIGN**
Eisenstrasse 31
Duesseldorf NRW 40227
Germany
+49 211 7 333 290
+49 211 7 952 441
mail@ninadavid.de

16, 17, **NOON**
122, 172 592 Utah Street
San Francisco, CA 94110 USA
415.621.4922
415.621.4966
info@designatnoon.com

221 **Ó!**
Klapparstíg 16
Reykjavik 101 Iceland
+354 562 3300
+354 562 3300
einar@oid.is

190 **OAKLEY DESIGN STUDIOS**
519 SW Park Ave., Ste 405
Portland, OR 97205 USA
503.241.3705
503.241.3812
oakleyds@oakleydesign.com

19, 29, **OCTAVO DESIGN**
81 130 Kerr Street
Fitzroy Australia
+613 9417 6022
+613 9417 6255
info@octavodesign.com.au

177 **OFFICE FOR DESIGN**
13B Nicolson House,
107 Nicolson Street
Brooklyn, Pretoria, Gauteng
South Africa
+27 12 346 7075
+27 12 343 4006
paula@officefordesign.co.za

17 **PARAGON MARKETING
COMMUNICATIONS**
P. O. Box 6097
Salmiya, 22071 Kuwait
+965 600 99 77
+965 571 59 85
Louai@paragonmc.com

64 **PAVONE**
1006 Market St.
Harrisburg, PA 17101 USA
717.234.8886
717.234.8940
rsmith@pavone.net

233 **PENGUINCUBE**
P. O. Box 113-6117, Hamra 1103
2100
Beirut Lebanon
+961 3 937305
tammam@penguincube.com

76 **PENTAGRAM DESIGN/SF**
387 Tehama Street
San Francisco, CA 94103 USA
415.896.0499
415.541.9106
lawson@sf.pentagram.com

52, 53, **PH.D**
80, 106, 1524A Cloverfield Blvd.
129, 179, Santa Monica, CA 90404 USA
199 310.829.0900
310.829.1859
phd@phdla.com

154, 228 **PIERRE RADEMAKER DESIGN**
738 Higuera St. Suite F
San Luis Obispo, CA 93401 USA
805.544.7774
805.544.0832
lg@rademakerdesign.com

37, 72, **PING-PONG DESIGN**
198 Rochussenstraat 400
3015 ZC Rotterdam
The Netherlands
+31(0) 10 436 57 44
+31 (0) 10 436 45 60
info@pingpongdesign.com

228 **PINXIT**
Via Salata 9/11
16121 Genova
010 5451435
010 8680843
erigoli@pinxit.it

84, 202, **PLAZM**
212 P. O. Box 2863
Portland, OR 97208 USA
503.528.8000
503.528.8092
josh@plazm.com

132, 178 **POULIN & MORRIS INC.**
180 286 Spring St., 6th Floor
New York, NY 10013 USA
212.675.1332
212.675.3027
info@poulinmorris.com

22, 23, **PUBLIC**
148, 186 10 Arkansas St./L
San Francisco, CA 94107 USA
415.863.2541
415.863.8954
lindsay@publicdesign.com

40, 173 **PUNCHCUT**
130 Bush St. 8th Flr.
San Francisco, CA 94104 USA
415.445.8855
415.445.8857
benson@punchcut.com

182 **Q**
Sonnenberger Str. 16
Wiesbaden, 65193 Germany
0049-611-18 13 10
0049-611-18 13 118
info@q-home.de

62 **RED DOG DESIGN
CONSULTANTS**
40 Lower Kevin Street
Dublin 8 Ireland
(00353) 1476 0180
(00353) 1418 9820
mary.doherty@reddog.ie

61, 226 **RED HERRING DESIGN**
75 Varick Street Rm. 1508
New York, NY 10013 USA
212.219.0557
212.219.0720
cb@rhdnyc.com

106, 145, **RICK JOHNSON & COMPANY**
203 1120 Pennsylvania NE
Albuquerque NM 87110 USA
505.266.1100
505.262.0525
tmcgrath@rjc.com

61 **RICOCHET CREATIVE
THINKING**
319 Crichton Street
Ottawa, ON Canada
613.789.5232
613.789.5317
steve@ricochetcreativethin
king.ca

114 **RIORDON DESIGN**
131 George Street
Oakville, ON L6J 3B9 Canada
905.339.0750
905.339.0753
group@riordondesign.com

56, 68 **SABET BRANDS**
1760 Kaiser Ave.
Irvine, CA 92614 USA
949.395.8134
ali@sabet.com

65, 139, **SAGMEISTER INC.**
167 222 West 14 Street
New York, NY 10011 USA
212.647.1789
212.647.1788
stefan@sagmeister.com

143, 177 **SALT BRANDING**
30 Hotaling Place, 1st Floor
San Francisco, CA 94111 USA
415.616.1515
415.362.3495
cesar@saltsf.com

107 **SALVA O'RENICK**
511 Delaware, Suite 1
Kansas City, MO 64105 USA
816.842.6996
816.842.6989
mpaoletti@uncommonsense
.com

DIRECTORY

34, 36, 62, 105   SIMON & GOETZ DESIGN
Westhafen Pier 1, Rotfeder-
Ring 11
60327 Frankfurt/Main Germany
+49 (0) 69 968855 0
+49 (0) 69 968855 23
a.hellweg@simongoetz.de

85, 229   SKY DESIGN
50 Hurt Plaza, Suite 500
Atlanta, GA 30303 USA
404.688.4702
404.688.2255
skydesign@at.asdnet.com

56   SPARC, INC.
824 Humboldt Ave.
Winnetka, IL 60093 USA
847.784.3100
847.784.3101
rcassis@sparcinc.com

171   ST. IVES/CREATIVE SIDE
13449 NW 42 Ave.
Miami, FL 33054 USA
305.685.7381 ext. 457
305.685.3448
jeff.kincaid@stivescreative.com

20   STOLLER DESIGN GROUP
1818 Harmon St.
Berkeley, CA 94703 USA
510.658.9771
510.658.9772
tia@planetstoller.com

59, 165   STUDIO SONSOLES LLORENS
CASP 56 4° DCHA
08010 Barcelona Spain
+34 934 124 171
+34 934 124 298
info@sonsoles.com

47, 93, 220   STUDIO A
Salaverry 3328
Lima 17 Peru
511 264 2886
511 264 2891
v.majluf@studioa.com.pe

70, 208   SUBPLOT DESIGN INC.
301-318 Homer Street
Vancouver BC V6B 2V2 Canada
604.685.2990
604.685.2909
info@subplot.com

175   UMUT SÜDÜAK
Gorimuntarpasa Sok. No: 45/29
Istanbul 34724 Turkey
+90 216 414 9948
+90 216 478 4969
usuduak@tnn.net

73, 144   SULLIVANPERKINS
2811 McKinney Ave. Suite 320
Dallas, TX 75039 USA
214.922.9080
214.922.0044
jarrod.holt@sullivanperkins
.com

66   SUSSNER DESIGN COMPANY
212 3rd Avenue North, Suite 505
Minneapolis, MN 55401 USA
612.339.2886
612.339.2887
derek@sussner.com

92, 105, 158, 159   TALISMAN INTERACTIVE
4169 Main Street, Suite 200
Philadelphia, PA 19127 USA
215.482.6600 ext. 223
215.482.0600
mmcdonald@talismaninter
active.com

57   TANAGRAM PARTNERS
855 West Blackhawk
Chicago, IL 60622 USA
312.787.6831
312.787.6834
info@tanagram.com

97   TEMALIDESIGN
61 Russell Road
Albany, NY 12205 USA
518.265.2478
terri@temalidesign.com

25, 187, 207   TEMPLIN BRINK DESIGN
720 Tehama Street
San Francisco, CA 94103 USA
415.255.9295
415.255.9296
jtemplin@tbd-sf.com

30   THE JONES GROUP
342 Marietta St. NW #3
Atlanta, GA 30313 USA
404.523.2606
404.522.6187
vicky@thejonesgroup.com

121   TILKA DESIGN
921 Marquette Ave., Suite #200
Minneapolis, MN 55402 USA
612.664.8994
612.664.8991
jtilka@tilka.com

150   TIM SMITH DESIGN
6864 Shamrock Circle
Loveland, OH 45140 USA
513.519.8919
614.559.6529
tsmith@timsmithdesign.com

124, 214   TRACY DESIGN
118 S. W. Blvd.
Kansas City, MO 64108 USA
816.421.0606
816.421.0177
jan@tracydesign.com

66   TREIBSTOFF WERBUNG
Lohbergstr. 76
Herdecke 58313 Germany
+49 2330 8032 812
+49 2330 8032 810
bielicki@treibstoff-werbung.de

225   TRUMPET
839 St. Charles Ave.
New Orleans, LA 70130 USA
205.401.8001
ness@iamalwayshungry.com

56   TURNER DUCKWORTH
831 Montgomery St.
San Francisco, CA 94133 USA
415.675.7777
415.675.7778
joanne@turnerduckworth.com

101   TYPE G
130 South Cedros Ste 3
Solana Beach, CA 92075 USA
858.792.7333
858.792.8733
miken@typegdesign.com

51, 69, 166, 190   UP DESIGN BUREAU
209 East William, Suite 1100
Wichita, KS 67202 USA
316.267.1546
316.267.3760
cp@updesignbureau.com

87, 137, 145, 234   VERLANDER DESIGN
P.O. Box 370156
Montara, CA 94037 USA
online@verlanderdesign.com

102   VINEGAR HILL PRINTERS, LLC
170 Tillary St. #506
Brooklyn, NY 11201 USA
718.858.7379
amelia@vinegarhillprinters
.com

58, 151, 181, 211   VOICE
217 Gilbert Street
Adelaide SA 5000 Australia
618 8410 8822
618 8410 8933
info@voicedesign.net

28   VRONTIKIS DESIGN OFFICE
2707 Westwood Blvd.
Los Angeles, CA 90064 USA
310.446.5446
310.446.5456
pv@35k.com

40, 45, 54, 55   WATTS DESIGN
66 Albert Road
South Melbourne, Victoria,
3205 Australia
61 3 9696 4116
61 3 9696 4006
peter@wattsdesign.com.au

163   JOEL WASSERMAN
P. O. Box 442
Sydney NSW 1360 Australia
+61 411226467
joel@gwarsh.com

78, 177   WEMAKE DESIGN
2 Janeville, Off St. Kevins
Parade, Dublin 8, Ireland
353 1 4738498
nik@wemakedesign.com

142   WILLOUGHBY DESIGN GROUP
602 Westport Rd.
Kansas City, MO 64111 USA
816.561.4189
816.561.5052
slee@willoughbydesign.com

18, 31, 115, 226   WOW! BRANDING
101-1300 Richards
Vancouver, BC V6B 3G6 Canada
604.683.5655
866.877.4032
tara@wowbranding.com

118   XMI DESIGN
The Malting Tower, Grand Canal
Quay
Dublin 2 Ireland
00 353 1 661 7600
00 3531 661 7610
denis@xmi.ie

71   Y & R
303 2nd Street, 8th Floor
San Francisco, CA 94107 USA
415.882.0600
415.882.0745
chris_rooney@sfo.yr.com

DIRECTORY

Thank you.

A debt of gratitude is owed to the following:

Amelie Wen
Judge, Statistician, Partner

Tim Belonax
Designer, Inquisitor, Advocate

Cindy Wang
Recorder

Kristin Ellison (Rockport)
Editor, Initiator

Regina Grenier (Rockport)
Coordinator, Encourager, Elevator